DATE DUE

LEADERSHIP SKILLS HANDBOOK

D0711549

THE LEADERSHIP SKILLS HANDBOOK

50 key skills from 1,000 leaders

Jo Owen

KOGAN PAGE

London and Philadelphia

Publisher's note

Every possible effort has been made to ensure that the information contained in this book is accurate at the time of going to press, and the publishers and author cannot accept responsibility for any errors or omissions, however caused. No responsibility for loss or damage occasioned to any person acting, or refraining from action, as a result of the material in this publication can be accepted by the editor, the publisher or the author.

First published in Great Britain and the United States in 2006 by Kogan Page Limited

120 Pentonville Road
London N1 9JN
United Kingdom
www.kogan-page.co.uk

525 South 4th Street, #241
Philadelphia PA 19147
USA

© Jo Owen, 2006

ISBN-10 0 7494 4827 X
ISBN-13 978 0 7494 4827 1

British Library Cataloguing-in-Publication Data

A CIP record for this book is available from the British Library.

Library of Congress Cataloging-in-Publication Data

Owen, Jo.
The leadership skills handbook : 50 key skills from 1000 real leaders / Jo Owen.
p. cm.
Includes bibliographical references.
ISBN 0-7494-4827-X
1. Leadership--Handbooks, manuals etc. 2. Management--Handbooks, manuals, etc. I. Title
HD57.7.O947 2006
658.4'092--dc22
2006013353

Typeset by Jean Cussons Typesetting, Diss, Norfolk
Printed and bound in the Great Britain by MPG Books Ltd, Bodmin, Cornwall

Contents

Acknowledgements

This book reflects the collective knowledge, wisdom and experience of thousands of leaders who have contributed through surveys, interviews and real experience. I am especially grateful to the outstanding leaders of the future at Teach First who have effectively tested and challenged many of the ideas in this book. Our future is in good hands when they do emerge as our leaders. Monitor Group kindly provided some of the initial research that provoked the new thinking and insights behind this book.

I would not have written the book without the encouragement of Jon Finch at Kogan Page. Professor Nigel Nicholson at London Business School generously gave time, insight and hospitality; Dr Nick Baylis at Cambridge University has opened up whole new vistas on leadership through his positive psychology work; Francis Gouillart and Professor Venkat Ramaswamy at Michigan Business School have also opened new doors through their co-creation work. The staff at Teach First have quietly worked wonders on some of my leadership efforts, in particular Susie Currie, James Townsend, Laura Donovan and Brett Wigdortz. The faults in this book are all mine: I could not have wished for better support and insight from such a wonderful group of people.

Most importantly, I would like to thank those many organizations for which I have worked across the world. There is no substitute for seeing leadership in action: it is never as simple as it looks in books. So my thanks go to:

ABN Amro
Accenture
AIG
American Express
Apple Computers
Armstrong Industries
Aviva
Barclays Bank
BT
Cap Gemini
Central Bank of Indonesia
Chase Group
Citigroup
Crown Prosecution Service
Diatech
EDS
Hallmark Cards
HBOS
HCA
ICI
ItoChu
Leadership Partnership
Lloyds TSB
MAC Group
Merita Nordbanken
Merrill Lynch
MetLife
Mitsubishi Chemicals
Monsanto
National Air Traffic Services
NCB
Netfoods
NHS
Norwegian Dairy Association
Peoples Choice
Philips
Procter & Gamble
RBS
RHM
Royal Sun Alliance
SABIC
San Miguel
SDP
Start Up
SWIFT
Teach First
Territory Mapping
Thorn Rental
UBS
Union Carbide
Young Entrepreneurs' Organization
ZFS

Introduction

Most leadership books try to answer the question 'What is good leadership?' That is like trying to answer the question 'What are people like?' The resulting debate generates more heat than light because leaders, like people, come in many different shapes and sizes.

This handbook is different. It starts with the question 'How can you learn to lead?' In our research with over a thousand leaders at all levels in the public, private and voluntary sectors, one thing was clear: leaders learn not from courses but from experience, bosses, peers and role models. Some of the lessons are positive: we try to copy effective behaviour. Some lessons are negative: we see a boss or peer explode spectacularly and quietly decide not to copy that mistake.

The problem with learning from experience is that it is a random walk. Bump into good role models and experiences and you learn good lessons. Get the wrong role models and experience and you learn the wrong lessons. Not many people become leaders through the luck of the random walk.

This handbook will help you take the randomness out of the random walk of experience. It gives you a framework for observing and learning from the experiences you go through. The structure lets you learn faster than your peers: this is your guide to accelerated leadership.

Our research identified the main practical skills that leaders must have. No leader gets ticks in all the boxes. But you need to develop some signature strengths, and you do not want to fail badly in any area.

The book does not prescribe a single formula for success. You will not have to become Nelson Mandela, Genghis Khan or Mother Teresa to succeed. The book allows you to create your own formula for success. Your success formula will reflect a combination of what works in your sector, organization and profession plus what works for you as an individual.

The leadership riddle

There are two dead-end roads to leadership. The first dead end is to try to be someone else. We cannot be Churchill, Gandhi and Alexander the Great all rolled into one (although there are some people who think they are already that good). We have to be true to ourselves.

The other dead end is simply to be who we are, in the vain hope that the world will recognize our innate brilliance and leadership talent. We could land up waiting a very long time.

So now we have a problem: we cannot become leaders by being someone else, and we cannot succeed by being who we are. How do we solve this riddle?

The solution is that we have to become the best of who we are. This book is your guide to discovering how to be the best of who you are. It will help you discover, build and celebrate your strengths. You will not have to sacrifice your personality: you can be a leader on your own terms, not on the terms of some guru with a great theory.

This handbook features the core skills leaders need to develop. Each skill has a framework to help you think about how that skill should be deployed ideally. Just as importantly, each skill has some blank space. This is where you should record examples of where you saw the skill being deployed well or less well. You should think hard about why it was effective or less effective. As you observe and record real-life examples of skills in action, you will be developing your own unique formula for success in your own unique context.

Use this book as your personal leadership coach. Do not try to read it cover to cover. Use individual chapters when the need arises. Ideally, use it before an event to decide how to deal with it. After the event, reflect on what worked and did not work: build up your personal perspectives on what leadership practices work for you.

This handbook is to be used by you to create your own leadership DNA. Ideal leadership is always inferior to practical leadership: what works for you where you are. The handbook only succeeds if you use it as an active tool. When you are faced with an unfamiliar challenge, refer back to this handbook and your notes. Use the book well and it can become your personal guide and coach on the road to leadership.

Whatever your journey is, enjoy it.

Part 1

Career skills

Section 1
Understand yourself

As a leader, understanding yourself does not require seeing a guru in India, gazing at your navel or discussing your childhood with a shrink. It requires that you understand how you affect other people.

Do not worry about what box shrinks try to put you in. Boxes are for the dead, not the living. You only need to worry about how you affect others. If you understand this, then you understand what matters about yourself.

Next, you need some way of understanding yourself and how you affect others, without calling a shrink or your new-age guru. For better or for worse, there are many psychological tools to help you or, in some cases, confuse and depress you.

The Myers-Briggs Type Indicator (MBTI) is very much the tool du jour. It takes many years to become an expert at it, which defeats its own purpose. The idea is not to become an MBTI expert: it is to become a leader.

The received wisdom about all these models, including MBTI, is that there is no 'bad' category. This is a useful fiction used by facilitators who want an easy time with the groups they lead. Like the astrologers who always give positive horoscopes, they do not want to upset paying customers. All the categories in MBTI have a positive side and a negative side. You affect people both positively and negatively with your style, and it pays to understand both sides.

Table 1.1 shows a revisionist version of MBTI.

Table 1.1 Myers–Briggs Type Indicator (MBTI) outline

Type	Description	Positive Impact	Negative Impact
Extroversion (E)	Gains energy from others. Speaks, then thinks.	Spreads energy, enthusiasm.	Loudmouth. Does not include other people.
Introversion (I)	Gains energy from within. Thinks before speaking.	Thoughtful. Gives space to others.	Nothing worth saying? Uneasy networker.
Sensing (S)	Observes outside world. More facts, fewer ideas.	Practical, concrete, detailed.	Dull, unimaginative.
Intuitive (N)	Pays attention to self, inner world, ideas.	Creative, imaginative.	Flighty, impractical, unrealistic.
Thinking (T)	Decides with head and logic.	Logical, rational, intellectual.	Cold and heartless.
Feeling (F)	Listens to the heart.	Empathetic, understanding.	Soft-headed, fuzzy thinker, bleeding heart.
Judging (J)	Organized, scheduled, tidy.	High work ethic. Focused and reliable.	Compulsive neat freak. Uptight, rigid, rule-bound.
Perceiving (P)	Keeps options open. Opportunistic.	Work-life balance. Enjoys work.	Lazy, messy, aimless and unreliable.

Exercise 1.1:
Discovering your style

Your first exercise is to figure out where you are on MBTI.

As you look at the list of positive characteristics, you will naturally believe you have all of them. You will discover the truth you long suspected: you are perfect. MBTI does not let you off so lightly. You have to choose between E and I, between S and N, between T and F and between J and P. The result is that in the world of MBTI you become an ugly acronym like ENTP, or ISFJ, or INFP.

If you are still having difficulty discovering your style, look at the negative impact column in the MBTI chart. You will probably discover quickly what you are least like.

Now do the same for your boss. Putting him or her in the right negative boxes is pretty easy for most people.

Boxes are for the dead, not the living.

NOTES

_____

_____

_____

_____

_____

_____

_____

_____

Section 2
Understand others

The pay-off from going through MBTI comes when you use it to influence others effectively.

A good team will be a mix of styles. If everyone is an introvert, the room will echo to the sound of silence. If everyone is an extrovert the room will be rowdier than a chimpanzees' tea party. These odd combinations are productive, but hard to maintain. A common trade-off is between the Thinking types and the Feeling types. Thinkers often focus only on tasks and actions; feelers will speak of little other than people. You need a team that can manage both the tasks and the people, and you need to recognize that the different styles of each team member are valuable. Table 1.2 shows how to deal with the different types of person.

There are a few principles hidden in here:

■ *Do not try to be someone else.*
  If you are an introvert, then you are not suddenly going to transform yourself into an extrovert who is the life and soul of the party. Under stress, people often do resort to a second style of operation. This is often catastrophic: they have had less practice at that style so they are operating with a rarely used style in a high-stress situation. The outcome is rarely good. Be true to yourself.
■ *Do not try to change the other person.*
  Understand how the other person's style differs from yours. These differences are positive. Together, you are likely to be able to achieve more than if you operate independently. An intuitive person will have many ideas and a sensing person will be very practical on the detail. One of you is the guru with the vision; the other is the commissar who can work out how to make the vision real. It is a powerful leadership combination.
■ *Be patient.*
  If you are highly task-focused (T) it can be frustrating if someone else never talks about the critical tasks in hand.

Table 1.2 Myers–Briggs Type Indicator (MBTI) outline

Your Type	Their Type	How They May See You	How You Can Adjust
Extroversion (E)	Introvert	Loudmouth. Does not include other people.	Give others time to think and to speak. Ask open questions.
Introversion (I)	Extrovert	Nothing worth saying? Uneasy networker.	Prepare in advance to have something to say.
Sensing (S)	Intuitive	Dull, unimaginative.	Take over some of the practical detail that intuitive types dislike.
Intuitive (N)	Sensing	Flighty, impractical, unrealistic.	Ask for help on practical things: form an alliance with a sensing person.
Thinking (T)	Feeling	Cold and heartless.	Try to win a friend, not just win an argument.
Feeling (F)	Thinking	Soft-headed, fuzzy thinker, bleeding heart.	Let the thinkers think; then work the people and the politics.
Judging (J)	Perceiving	Compulsive neat freak. Uptight, rigid, rule-bound.	Ignore the chaos; quietly focus on the substantive battles.
Perceiving (P)	Judging	Lazy, messy, aimless and unreliable.	Clear up the mess on the desk and make sure the report gets in on time.

Instead this person talks about people the whole time. The person is an F. This is a good combination: one of you works out what needs to be done (T); the other works the politics and people (F) to enable it to happen.

■ *Be aware.*
Most of us stumble into personal and professional relationships. We know how long it takes to build personal relationships. We have little time to build professional relationships. We need to understand other people's styles fast so that we can influence them positively and quickly.

■ *Find the right situation in which to work.*
Warren Buffet remarked that, 'when a great manager joins a lousy company, it is normally the reputation of the company that remains intact'. The same is true of work styles: you will not change the style of the organization in which you work. You need to find a way of living with the style of your organization, or you need a new organization.

■ *Build the team.*
Strong teams are diverse. Diversity does not mean regulatory diversity and having token minorities decorating the cover of the annual report. It means the subtler diversity of building a team with complementary styles, skills and perspectives. A football team of 11 goalkeepers is unlikely to do well.

When a great manager joins a lousy company, it is normally the reputation of the company that remains intact.

A football team of 11 goalkeepers is unlikely to do well.

NOTES

Section 3
Understand how you affect others

Leadership requires getting other people to do things. It often means getting others to do things they would rather not do: for some people, working for you may not be as attractive as having a family life and meeting friends.

Some leaders think you lead by coercion. Coercion can be remarkably effective in the short term. When a mugger held a knife to my neck and asked for my money, I duly obliged. The mugger made me do something I preferred not to do, but he was not an ideal leadership role model. He had achieved compliance, not commitment. Coercion and compliance were standard leadership models in the 19th century when bosses bossed and workers worked. In the 21st century there is a better-educated and more demanding workforce, which requires a different form of leadership. We all have suffered at the hands of bosses who are still stuck in the 19th century. Bossing people is lazy leadership. Increasingly, it is ineffective leadership.

To be an effective leader, you need to move beyond coercion and compliance. You need to be able to gain the commitment and support of the people you lead. You cannot gain their commitment if you do not understand them and you do not understand how you affect them.

We have seen from MBTI that understanding people can be a full-time profession. In practice, we do not have time to do a full psychological audit of each person we meet. As practising leaders, we need some short cuts to help us make sense of who we are meeting and how they are behaving.

The Style Compass™ is a quick and easy way of thinking about how to influence someone. In this exercise, think of someone you are trying to influence. You should get plenty of practice with your boss, so try him or her.

Exercise 1.2:
The Style Compass

The first step is to decide what are the important aspects of the person's character.

Here are some typical characteristics that practising leaders have identified as being important in the people they deal with:

- people-focused versus task-focused;
- process-focused versus outcome-focused;
- risk-tolerant versus risk-averse;
- big picture versus detail;
- words versus numbers;
- oral versus written communication;
- inductive versus deductive;
- tactful versus blunt;
- sensitive versus thick-skinned;
- controlling versus empowering;
- quick versus slow;
- open versus defensive;
- morning versus afternoon;
- positive versus cynical;
- analysis versus action.

Here are a few more dimensions that different shrinks believe are important. You decide what counts in your context. These dimensions have considerable analytical rigour behind them, and each branch of psychology promotes its own set of dimensions as being the only true, meaningful and relevant dimensions. You decide which ones you find most useful:

- intellectual versus instinctual;
- withdrawn versus attached;
- idealistic versus practical;
- alert versus settled;
- progressive versus conservative;
- non-traditional versus traditional;
- future-oriented versus past-oriented;
- congenial versus coercive;

- solicitous versus antagonistic;
- receptive versus assertive;
- submissive versus domineering;
- acceptance-seeking versus pleasure-seeking;
- sensitive versus insensitive;
- socialistic versus materialistic.

Step two is to plot the person's characteristics on the Compass, as illustrated in Figure 1.1.

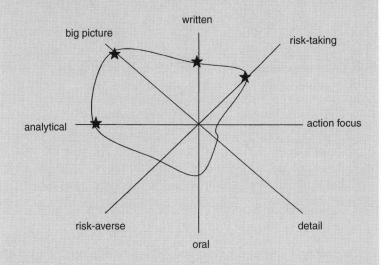

Figure 1.1   The Style Compass for my boss

As you plot the Style Compass, focus on what is most important about the other person, not about yourself. The dimensions can be anything you think is most important. In this case, the stars show I think my boss is very analytical, likes the big picture, is a risk taker and prefers written communications.

Step three is to plot yourself on your boss's Style Compass (see Figure 1.2). If you are well aligned you are lucky. More likely, you will have to figure out how to get on to his or her wavelength.

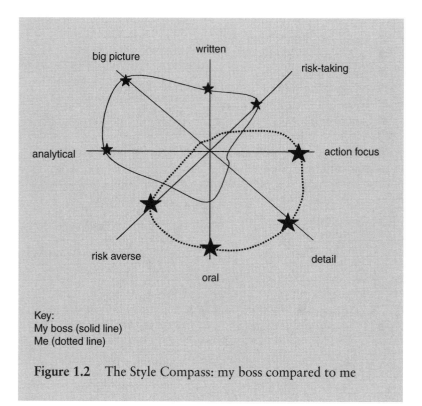

Figure 1.2 The Style Compass: my boss compared to me

In the example above, my boss and I are very different. This could make us a very effective but difficult working combination. After drawing this Style Compass, I realize that I need to adapt to get on the wavelength of my boss. I need to produce more written material: the boss feels more comfortable with that than with oral briefings. I just need to focus on the big picture, and be sure to give plenty of analytical reasons why the big picture is the right one. I also need to curb my instinct to plunge into doing lots of practical things until the big picture has been agreed: otherwise, the boss will think I may be wasting my time doing the wrong thing. Naturally, I think the boss is wasting time analysing all the big stuff when we could be moving to action. When I am the boss, things will change. But in the meantime, I get to play by the boss's rules, not mine.

The mugger was not an ideal leadership role model. He had achieved compliance, not commitment.

NOTES

_____

_____

_____

_____

_____

_____

_____

_____

_____

_____

_____

_____

_____

_____

_____

_____

_____

_____

_____

Section 4
Discover your rules of success

The rules of success and survival change depending on your organization and its circumstances. Think of risk taking: it is the lifeblood of an investment bank and it is like kryptonite to the Civil Service. In one context, you cannot survive without risk taking; in the other, risk taking kills you.

This is a critical, and deceptively difficult, exercise for you.

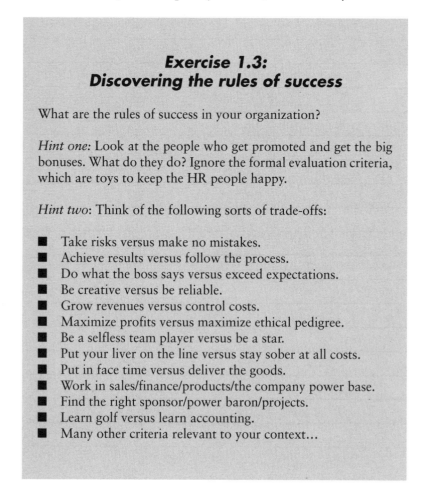

Exercise 1.3:
Discovering the rules of success

What are the rules of success in your organization?

Hint one: Look at the people who get promoted and get the big bonuses. What do they do? Ignore the formal evaluation criteria, which are toys to keep the HR people happy.

Hint two: Think of the following sorts of trade-offs:

■ Take risks versus make no mistakes.
■ Achieve results versus follow the process.
■ Do what the boss says versus exceed expectations.
■ Be creative versus be reliable.
■ Grow revenues versus control costs.
■ Maximize profits versus maximize ethical pedigree.
■ Be a selfless team player versus be a star.
■ Put your liver on the line versus stay sober at all costs.
■ Put in face time versus deliver the goods.
■ Work in sales/finance/products/the company power base.
■ Find the right sponsor/power baron/projects.
■ Learn golf versus learn accounting.
■ Many other criteria relevant to your context...

You may not like the rules of success in your organization. Selling your soul to succeed may not be worth it. If you do not like the rules of success, do not complain about them. Save your breath. You can adapt, or leave, or sulk.

> **Sulking is not a good route to leadership.**

NOTES

_____

_____

_____

_____

_____

_____

_____

_____

_____

_____

_____

_____

_____

Section 5
The leadership journey: key principles

Your potential is defined by your ambition and your ability (see Figure 1.3).

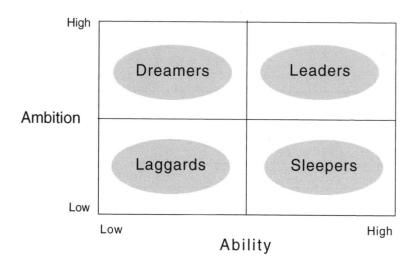

Figure 1.3 Leadership success matrix

For a moment, we will assume that, since you have bought this book and taken the trouble to read this far, you are showing the sort of ambition required of a leader. People with low ambition are unlikely to read this book. So you can put yourself in the upper half of the diagram above.

We can, naturally, also assume that you are talented. The only real question is whether you are developing the right sort of talent to be an effective leader.

Schools teach exactly the wrong sorts of skills for becoming a leader. In school you are working *by yourself* to *predetermined goals* where there is an intellectually correct answer. Any aspiring leader who waits to be set goals, thinks all the answers are rational and works alone is unlikely to succeed. Leadership requires crafting an agenda (setting goals, not just accepting them), working in a deeply political world and working closely with other people. School does not teach this. Business school fails dismally to teach this. And most corporate training swings wildly between technical training (accounting and systems) and tree hugging, raft building and team building on the other side.

In reality, you cannot be taught to lead. You have to discover how to lead through experience and observation.

To help you structure your leadership journey, look at Figure 1.4. This is your entire leadership career laid out before you.

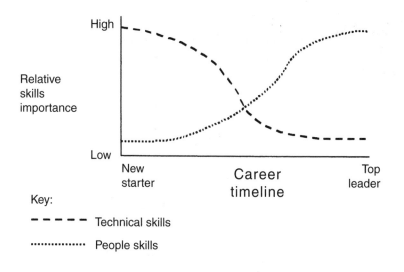

Figure 1.4 The leader's skills and career

Most people start their careers learning some basic technical skills. This trade craft is unique to each trade: accounting, law, IT, financial analysis, psychology or dealing in the tripartite asset collaterized repo market. You can make small fortunes through technical skills: Premiership footballers are highly skilled and highly paid, but they are not leaders.

Technical skills are a trap. Many people see promotion as an opportunity to deal with more complex technical problems and to solve the technical problems that beat other people. That is not leadership: leadership requires getting other people to do things. It is not about doing it all yourself. The CEO cannot solve every problem in the organization from unfreezing your computer screen to dealing with the VAT inspector.

Leaders all develop strong people skills. People skills cover a myriad of capabilities covered in this book: delegating, motivating, influencing, resolving conflict, building teams, setting goals and leading change.

For any aspiring leader, the challenge is to develop the people skills early: it is easier to experiment, mess up and change early in your career than when you find yourself suddenly leading an organization with over 1,000 people in it. Some organizations develop these people skills fast: the armed forces, teaching and many service sector jobs such as hotels, restaurants and clubs provide unique training grounds in dealing with the human animal.

Exercise 1.4:
Are you on the right journey?

1. Are you learning great technical skills (dealing in bonds, accounting, law), which lead to a profession or to middle management?
2. Are you also learning how to get people to do things: delegating, coaching, resolving conflict, motivating, persuading, selling a vision and direction and leading? This is the road to leadership.

> **Schools teach exactly the wrong sorts of skills for becoming a leader.**

NOTES

_____

_____

_____

_____

_____

_____

_____

_____

_____

_____

_____

_____

_____

_____

_____

_____

_____

_____

_____

_____

Section 6
Managing your leadership journey: the map

By now, it should be clear that leadership means different things to different people in different organizations. It also means different things at different levels of an organization. This can become truly confusing. But there is a way through this confusing jungle. Our research showed that, at each level of an organization, there are fundamentally different expectations of what a leader should look like and do. The differences are consistent across industries and countries, with some minor exceptions: in Japan they rate the ability to speak English as a key leadership requirement. If Anglo-Saxons could also learn to use English better, we would all be saved much drivel.

Take a look at Table 1.3. It shows the top five expectations of what a good leader looks like at each level of an organization. Note the following:

■ Respondents all believed that you can lead at all levels of the organization: leadership is not the sole preserve of the CEO. To succeed, you need to develop and practise leadership skills from an early stage.

■ Expectations of what good leaders look like change at each level. This explains why some people do very well at one level but then get altitude sickness at the next level. To succeed, you need to adapt to new rules of success at each level.

■ There is a large dissatisfaction with top leaders' ability to motivate others: only 37 per cent are satisfied with top leaders on this criterion.

■ The performance expectations for emerging leaders are low and largely about behaviour: hard work, proactivity, reliability. Many aspiring leaders fall over these very low hurdles.

■ The most divisive criterion was honesty and integrity. A boss who was rated well on this, and was therefore trusted, tended to be rated well on everything else. Bosses who rated poorly on this were damned on all other criteria.

Table 1.3 Top five expectations of leaders at all levels

Top Leaders	Leaders in the Middle	Recent Graduates/ Emerging Leaders
Vision (61%)	Ability to motivate others (43%)	Hard work (64%)
Ability to motivate others (37%)	Decisiveness (54%)	Proactivity (57%)
Decisiveness (47%)	Industry experience (70%)	Intelligence (63%)
Ability to handle crises (56%)	Networking ability (57%)	Reliability (61%)
Honesty and integrity (48%)	Delegation (43%)	Ambition (64%)

Note: Satisfaction ratings in brackets

The good news about these criteria is that you do not have to be superhuman to be a leader. The leadership requirements are simple and basic, and many people fail to live up to them. Focus on these basics, do them well and you will stand apart from many of your peer group.

> **You do not have to be superhuman to be a leader.**

NOTES

Section 7
Finding the right place at the right time

Polar bears are as useless in the African bush as a lion is in the Arctic.

The same principles apply to leadership. Leadership is contextual: leaders only succeed in the right context. Even Churchill had what he called his 'wilderness years': 20 years between the two world wars. The Second World War was his finest hour. When he was re-elected as prime minister in 1950, he was fairly useless as a peace-time leader. We all need the right context in which to succeed.

So how do you know if you are in the right place at the right time? Here are four tests for you to apply:

1. Is this an organization with prospects? A declining organization has fewer opportunities than a growing one. Are those prospects real and sustainable? How does the organization compare to its peer group?
2. Will I enjoy the work? You only excel at what you enjoy. And you will spend a large part of your waking hours at work. So if you are working just for the money, you will find it tough to sustain the enthusiasm and stamina required on the road to leadership.
3. What will I learn? You will learn some technical skills. But you will also need to learn people skills and leadership skills. Are you learning the right mix of skills to sustain the leadership journey, or are you simply reinforcing technical skills, which will keep you at your current level?
4. How will this experience look on my CV? Will other employers value the skills and experience I am gaining, or am I locking myself into my current employer by acquiring a very narrow set of skills and experience?

If you answer these questions and feel an urge to rush off and join another organization, be careful. The grass may be greener on the other side of the hill. Where it is greenest is where it rains most.

Do not assume that other organizations are perfect. All organizations suffer from the same problems of politics, inadequate resources, shifting goals, ambiguous decision making, complex processes and a mixture of management talent from the great to the abysmal. Within an industry, the similarities are even greater. And when you do move, you immediately lose your power base, your relationships, your carefully nurtured credibility and trust, and your knowledge of how to make things happen in your complex and ambiguous world. In other words, you suddenly lose all the skills you need to be effective. And however bad your current boss is, remember that bosses rarely last for long: either you or they tend to move as the corporate carousel takes another turn.

> **Where it is greenest is where it rains most.**

NOTES

_____

_____

_____

_____

_____

_____

_____

_____

_____

_____

Section 8
Careers versus careering: avoiding the death stars

For some people, 'career' is a noun that describes a steady progression from fresh-faced graduate to a happy retirement. For others, 'career' is a verb that describes a chaotic slalom through myriad adventures on the path to leadership or disaster. Whether you want a career or prefer to career, it pays to avoid death star organizations, projects and bosses. Traditionally, these are known as CLM for good reasons: they are Career Limiting Moves.

Death star organizations

You take a huge gamble when you join an organization. You can improve the odds if you join an organization that is likely to grow and succeed. Put simply, there are more opportunities for promotion in an organization growing at 20 per cent a year than in one declining 20 per cent a year. Do your research. Today's winners may not be tomorrow's winners. Anyone joining a telecoms company around 1985 would have joined a fixed-line company, not any of the small start-ups selling mobiles that looked like bricks and weighed like bricks to loud-mouthed and loudly dressed property developers. There have been many more opportunities with the mobile companies than with fixed-line operators over the last 20 years.

Death star projects

Ask yourself two questions before taking on an assignment: 1) Is the assignment worthwhile? 2) Is the assignment set up for success?

A worthwhile assignment is one that has relevance and impact at least two levels up the organization (unless you are already the CEO). Ideally, it will also be close to the centre of power. Being asked to run the business in Japan is exciting, but after three years everyone back in your home country will have forgotten that you exist. Your new bosses will not know what promises were made when you left: fulfilling other people's promises to you will be very low on their list of priorities. Stay close to the centre of power.

An assignment is set up for success if it has the four following characteristics:

1. *The right sponsor*
   If the project is relevant to someone two levels up, that person will be actively promoting and supporting it. This makes it worthwhile, and politically it makes it more likely to succeed.
2. *The right problem*
   Politically, any CEO problem is the right problem because you know it will get the visibility and support to make it succeed. In practice, you need to use judgement. Spending a year fixing the wrong problem is not a good career investment.
3. *The right team and resources*
   If the assignment is under-resourced or understaffed, then it is clearly not a real priority; worse, it is not likely to succeed.
4. *The right process*
   Working against insane deadlines, needing double and triple checks before sneezing and testing either everything or nothing are not good success recipes.

Finally, consider whether you are the right person for the job. Doing competitive research on the Thai tapioca industry appeals to some people and some people are very good at that sort of thing. Do not be lured by the prospect of doing tapioca research on a tropical island: consider very carefully whether you will actually be able to deliver a great result.

Avoiding death star projects is not always easy. Here are some basic principles:

■ *Switch your radar on.*
   Keep on the lookout for what are the emerging assignments and opportunities. Talk to everyone: gossip is good.

■ *Assume the cloak of invisibility when a death star assignment looms.*
Make sure that you are very busy elsewhere. Start making yourself useful by volunteering to do things for bosses: do someone a favour. That person will appreciate it, and you will be curiously unavailable when the death star assignment is being staffed.

■ *Avoid succeeding too much at things you do not like.*
If you are really good at developing business cases to justify systems changes in the life insurance industry, you may find that your pigeonhole becomes a career coffin: you will not be allowed to do anything else.

■ *Make yourself very useful to people who have interesting assignments.*
Volunteer to do stuff for them. Express an active interest in the assignments you are interested in: they will then work the formal system to get you assigned.

■ *Last and least, work the formal assignment system.*
HR people will tell you how the assignment system works. Their rational world of assignment systems tends to be overwhelmed by the political reality of bosses fighting to get the best staff on to their books. Work the politics hard, but try to avoid upsetting the HR people too much in the process.

Death star bosses

Death star bosses come in four unpalatable flavours:

1. too strong;
2. too weak;
3. wrong taste;
4. wrong menu.

Too strong bosses

These are the Darth Vader types who demand your soul. There is some good news about them: they will look after their team very protectively. But the moment you flinch or you fail to deliver, you are dead meat. You are 100 per cent in or 100 per cent out. They tend to chew up and spit out team members at an alarming rate.

Too weak bosses

These may feel easy to work with. But at crunch time they are often unable to deliver on expectations around pay, promotions and assignments.

The wrong taste

The wrong taste may simply be a matter of two styles that are too alike (two introverts with nothing to say to each other or two egos that take up too much space in the room). Or it may be a problem of two conflicting styles that cannot work together. Do the Style Compass to figure out what it will take to succeed with a boss.

Wrong menu

Even if everything else is right about the boss, if he or she is working in the wrong part of the organization you will be in trouble. From your perspective, the wrong part of the organization is one where either you are unlikely to succeed or there is limited career progression.

Avoid succeeding too much at things you do not like.

NOTES

_____

_____

_____

_____

_____

_____

_____

Section 9
Assessing your next move

A career change is a huge leap. Find the right context and you can succeed. Find the wrong context and you will struggle.

The starting point is to know what you are looking for. A good coach will help you ask the right questions:

■ Can I see myself enjoying work at this new organization? Do I like the people and its purpose?

■ Is this organization likely to be a winner? Why? Will it grow and create opportunities for me as it grows? Growing organizations have more opportunities than static ones.

■ Am I likely to succeed here? Do I have the right skills/cultural fit? What happened to the cohort of five years ago?

■ Will I be learning skills that will be helpful to me longer-term? Do the skills give me options or do they tie me into one specific career journey?

Every career leap is a leap in the dark, however much research you do. You swap certainty for uncertainty. To shed some partial light on the future you should do the standard searches:

■ the company website, which gives the official version of what the company is looking for and what it aspires to;

■ a net search for features and articles about the company and its employees;

■ standard recruiting material, magazines and placement office material.

The most important thing is to talk to people who work there or have worked there or are in a competitor. You are likely to know someone who knows someone, so start networking (see Part 4, Section 10).

> **Every career leap is a leap in the dark.**

NOTES

_____

_____

_____

_____

_____

_____

_____

_____

_____

_____

_____

_____

_____

_____

_____

_____

_____

_____

_____

_____

_____

_____

Section 10
Running the leadership marathon

One eminent business school professor claims that leadership is not a sprint: it is a marathon run in a series of 400-metre sprints. This shows that he is clueless about how to run a marathon. But, fortunately, he has more insight around leadership than he does around marathons. With a few notable exceptions, who are normally successful entrepreneurs, it takes decades to reach a senior leadership position. Leaders, like actors, take many years to become an overnight success.

The question for all aspiring leaders is how to build and sustain the stamina required for the leadership marathon.

The strategic answer was hinted at in the last section: you only excel at what you enjoy. Life is too short to do things you hate, even if they pay well. You will eventually stress out, burn out and drop out to start your organic pig farm in Wales. That is not the road to leadership. Whatever you do, enjoy it. Even if you do not succeed on the leadership journey, at least you will have enjoyed the trip.

The deeper answer is to look after yourself. This is where we enter the murky waters of well-being gurus, lifestyle gurus and ultimately power crystals, healing and feng shui.

Exercise 1.5:
The stress test

- ■ Do you regularly work more than 50 hours a week?
- ■ Do you take less than four weeks' holiday a year?
- ■ Do you let work come into your holidays and social/home life?
- ■ Do you drink more than 12 units of alcohol a week (1 pint = 2 units)?

- Do you smoke or take any other drugs?
- Do you feel tired often and/or have trouble getting to sleep?
- Do you get lots of small illnesses?
- Do you have more responsibility than authority, or a lack of control?

Try to balance your life so that not too many answers are 'yes'.

'Work-life balance' is not code for letting people go off and start families. It is about allowing you to create and sustain the energy that will carry you to the top, not to the pig farm.

Equally, here are some obvious answers:

- *Diet*
  The right foods make a big difference. Some people use gluten-free diets and other exotica to draw attention to themselves and make others treat them specially. You do not need to be a crank. But a diet of grease burgers and chips is a heart attack on a plate: it is not worth it.

- *Exercise*
  Find something you enjoy. Imitating a hamster on a treadmill is not for everyone.

- *Enjoyment*
  All the leaders we researched clearly enjoyed what they did. If there is stress, it is in the middle of the organization, not at the top.

- *Relaxation*
  Most leaders are not one-dimensional. They tend to have active interests outside work, which may be physical (hiking, skiing, sailing), intellectual and cultural (arts, clubs) or social.

- *Sleep*
  Turn up to work drunk and you can expect to be fired. Turn up tired, and it is a badge of honour. But the effects of tiredness on decision making, reactions and self-awareness are just the same as the effects of drinking.

■ *Switch-off time*
Switch off the computer, text messages, phone, e-mail and all the other technology that imprisons you into a 24/7 work style. You do not have to work at 2 am while you are meant to be on holiday.

Find what works for you. Remember that, just as the mind controls the body, so the body controls the mind. Try clenching your fists and jaw and then relaxing them: the difference is immediate. Breathing exercises and mild meditation can work wonders.

The one thing that is a false solution is all the 'work-life balance' initiatives promoted by politicians and do-gooders. 'Work-life balance' is a shorthand for finding reasons to work less. The answer is not to avoid work: the answer is to find work that you enjoy, that leads you where you want to go and that has meaning and relevance to you. Leadership is hard work: you cannot short cut to leadership by working less.

You only excel at what you enjoy.

NOTES

_____

_____

_____

_____

_____

_____

_____

Part 2

People skills

Section 1
Delegating

People do not like delegating. It often means:

■ loss of personal control;
■ time 'wasted' explaining, coaching and correcting;
■ unexpected outcomes, and dilution of personal standards;
■ stress from loss of control.

Effective delegation frees your time to focus on where you add most value and helps develop the skills of your team. Failure to delegate traps you into doing low-level jobs.

How not to delegate

The easy way to work out how to delegate well is to reflect on the worst experiences you have suffered from poor delegation. Then do the opposite. Here is the delegation style of one boss from the Museum of Management Malpractice. For legal reasons we will let 'Jim' stay anonymous.

Jim would only delegate three sorts of activities:

■ Routine rubbish. Delegating the administrivia freed him to do the important things, like working out how to get promoted.
■ Hospital passes. Whenever he had a project going horribly wrong, he would delegate it to a subordinate as a 'development opportunity'. When the project duly collapsed, he would walk away and leave the subordinate crushed under the collapse.
■ Last-minute panics. Fridays were good days to avoid Jim. He would be thinking of the weekend and of all the work he had not done: time to delegate it all, especially if the deadline was Monday morning. Goodbye weekend, hello office.

Jim also had a unique style of delegation. He seemed to have three main principles:

■ Be vague about the objectives, and then change his mind several times in the course of the project. This would double the effort and halve the morale of the team.
■ Be vague about deadlines, but bring them forward by several days at the last moment just to keep everyone on their toes.
■ Be vague about the process in terms of how to do it, the support available, the critical path and the check points. This gave him carte blanche to interfere at will with sudden and extreme demands at any point in the process.

On no account would he ever discuss any of this with the team. He saw himself as a strong manager, which meant that he preferred to issue commands, preferably with elaborate detail around what the consequences of failure would look like.

Principles of effective delegation are:

■ Ensure clarity over the task and the eventual success criteria. Make the team summarize back to you what they think the task and outcomes are meant to be. Do not assume they have understood anything until they say it back to you.
■ Ensure people have enough skills and resources to complete the job: do not delegate too much too soon.
■ Be clear about how you want to work together (progress reports). Discuss concerns before you start.
■ Be available to help, but do not interfere all the time. When they ask for help, require that they suggest solutions so that they always learn.
■ Delegate meaningful projects, not just administrivia. Stretch people and they will rise to the challenge. Giving away mundane jobs only demotivates people.
■ Show faith and trust in the team: praise successes, and do not undermine them.

Remember, you may have delegated authority, but you cannot delegate away responsibility. You are still accountable for the outcomes.

Exercise 2.1:
Effective delegation

Review the tasks you undertake, and allocate each one to one of the four sections of the delegation chart in Table 2.1. Then act on the outcomes.

Table 2.1 Delegation chart

	Others Could Do This	*Only I Can Do This*
Very Important	*Delegate* – supervise and support closely.	*Take the lead* – involve others so they can learn and develop.
Less Important	*Delegate* – make sure you are delegating more than just the rubbish.	*Are you sure?* – could be a development opportunity for someone

As you fill in the chart, do not ask 'Are they capable of doing it today?' but ask 'Could they do it with enough help, support and supervision?' Your goal is not just to do the job, but also to stretch and develop your staff. You will be surprised by how much your team can achieve with the right support: people tend to rise or fall to the level of expectations set for them. So set high expectations and have the courage to delegate extensively. This has the added advantages of making your life easier and making you more popular with your team: they will see that you are trusting them and developing them.

People do not like delegating.

NOTES

_____

_____

_____

_____

_____

_____

_____

_____

_____

_____

_____

_____

_____

_____

_____

_____

_____

_____

_____

Section 2
Motivating

2.1 Motivating: Theory X and Theory Y

Many trees have been destroyed by the motivation industry. The less fortunate among us also have had to endure motivational workshops. This is where a man (it is usually a man) in a white suit whips the audience up into a frenzy of excitement that lasts for as long as it takes for the attendees to reach the car park on the way home. Motivation is where shrinks go mad with their academic theories. Have they not yet heard of chocolate?

To save you from the dangerous men in white coats or white suits, we will explore three theories of motivation and then look at how the theories work in practice.

Exercise 2.2:
Applying theory to your reality

Think of one of your bosses and decide whether he or she is an X type or Y type of person (see Table 2.2). Do the same for a few of your colleagues.

X and Y represent two ways of thinking about human motivation, as described in the classic *Human Side of Enterprise* by Douglas McGregor (1960, McGraw-Hill, New York). Now match the X- and Y-type categories to two different contexts: 1) a 19th-century sweatshop, with the workers paid piece rates and hired for their hands, not their heads, and clear, simple jobs with clear outcomes and targets; 2) a 21st-century service firm with high skills, ambiguity about how things should be done, and a need for workers to use their heads more than their hands.

Table 2.2 X types and Y types

Management Criteria	X-Type Manager	Y-Type Leader
Basis of Power	Formal authority	Authority and respect
Focus of Control	Process compliance	Outcomes, achievement
Communication Style	One-way: tell and do	Two-way: tell and listen
Success Criteria	Make no mistakes	Beat targets
Attention to Detail	High	Moderate
Ambiguity Tolerance	Minimal	Moderate
Political Ability	Moderate	High
Preferred Structure	Hierarchy	Network

It should be fairly clear that theory Y fits many, but not all, current work contexts. But, in practice, many bosses find it easier to use theory X: it looks tough, sounds good and is easy to deploy.

Think for a moment:

■ How do you prefer to be led?
■ How in practice do you lead other people?
■ What would you change?
■ How do your staff prefer to be led?

> **Avoid dangerous men in white coats or white suits.**

NOTES

2.2 Motivating: Maslow

We all have hopes and we all have fears. Good leaders know how to tap into those hopes and fears. This stunning piece of common sense was wrapped up into a nice psychological theory by Maslow, and is now known as Maslow's hierarchy of needs. His basic argument is that we are all needs junkies. As soon as we have satisfied our basic needs for food and shelter we start realizing we have other needs. This makes sense in the ordinary world. One hundred years ago no one really thought that telephones, televisions, computers, cars, refrigerators, games consoles, iPods and pepperoni pizzas were necessities. A short conversation with a modern teenager will quickly establish that life is impossible without these essentials.

In business, people are also needs junkies. People in a company near to bankruptcy want a leader who can remove fear and create job security. The leader of a big company is probably thinking of his knighthood and leaving a legacy before he is forgotten completely. People have different needs in different contexts.

To make the theory digestible, there are three versions of it in Figure 2.1:

1. The original version is marked in *italics*.
2. The leadership version is below the italics in normal typeface.
3. The simplified, revisionist version is in the oval shapes.

People climb the ladder from the bottom: they do not aspire to leave a legacy if they are still in fear of losing their jobs. Equally, as soon as they have achieved one level, they want to achieve the next level, as long as the leader can make it easy for them: we may all want to be famous footballers, but it does take quite a lot of work...

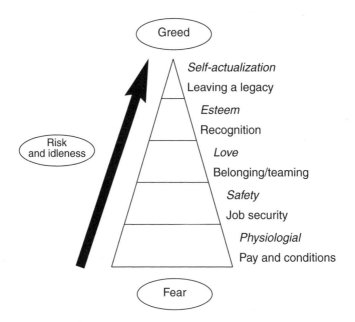

Figure 2.1 Maslow's hierarchy of needs (the unauthorized, revisionist, leadership version)

Exercise 2.3:
Motivating: Putting Maslow to work

1. Where are you on Maslow's hierarchy? Where do you want to get to? Will your current context allow you to get there? So what are you going to do about it?
2. In the next meeting you go to, see if you can spot where your colleagues are on the hierarchy. This may be difficult. So, in practice, use something simpler. As you persuade them to do something, work out if you are appealing to:
   - Their greed (hopes, ambitions, ability to complete a job).
   - Their fears (if they don't agree, the sky will fall down and they will not get promoted. If something is risky, they will resist. Show that the risk of doing nothing is greater than the risk of agreeing).

- Their idleness. Make it easy for them to agree, and awkward for them to disagree.
- What the risks are of doing something. If you can remove risk, you will make it much easier for them to agree with what you want.

As an exercise, always try to figure out how to appeal to fear, greed and idleness. Work out how to reduce the perceived risk of your idea. If people are resisting you, work out which of fear, greed, idleness and risk is out of balance.

3. Think of your top team member. Where is he or she on Maslow's hierarchy? What are the hopes you can play on? How can you raise expectations even further?

4. Think of your lowest-performing team member. Where is he or she on Maslow's hierarchy? What are this person's fears and concerns? What can you do to ease those fears and concerns?

We are all needs junkies.

Appeal to fear, greed and idleness.

NOTES

_____

_____

_____

_____

_____

2.3 Motivating: Management practice

Theory is good. Reality is better, or at least more useful, for leaders. Our research found five drivers of motivation. The good news is that none of the drivers are magical or difficult to understand (though they may be difficult to put into practice). They are common sense, which is why they are so rarely found in the workplace.

The drivers of motivation in the workplace are:

1. My boss shows an interest in my career.
2. I trust my boss: he or she is honest with me.
3. I know where we are going and how to get there.
4. I am doing a worthwhile job.
5. I am recognized for my contribution.

If your team agrees with the statements above, the chances are that they will also think you are smart and caring, have insight and are dynamic. They may even think you are witty and beautiful. If they disagree with the statements above, then they will damn you on all the other leadership criteria as well. Naturally, being seen to be a good boss with your team is not the same as impressing your bosses and delivering outstanding performance. But it is much easier to perform well with a team that supports and respects you than it is with a team that is alienated and demoralized.

Exercise 2.4:
Assess yourself
(and anyone else you want to)

Use these five drivers of motivation to assess yourself on how well you motivate. It may help to look in more detail at each driver:

1. *My boss shows an interest in my career:*
   – Do you know what ambitions your staff have?

- When did you last discuss their wants and needs informally?
- Have you made any compromises to support them (juggled priorities to let them go on training events/holidays etc)?

2. *My boss is honest with me:*
   - Do your staff really know how you rate them?
   - Do your staff know your personal and business priorities?

3. *We know where we are going and how to get there:*
   - Ask your staff to lay out the top three priorities for the next 3, 6 or 12 months. Are they the same as your priorities?

4. *Do your staff feel they are doing a worthwhile job?*
   - Are you delegating meaningful projects, or just administrivia?
   - Are your staff clearly stretched, are they cruising in their comfort zone or are they grumbling about meaningless chores?

5. *Are your staff recognized for their contribution?*
   - When was the last time you praised your team in public?
   - Do you let them star in front of senior management and other departments, or do you take the lead on all the big meetings?

When was the last time you praised your team in public?

NOTES

_____

_____

_____

Section 3
Selling

3.1 Selling: Features, benefits and dreams

Selling is not just for sales people. All leaders constantly have to sell themselves, sell their ideas and sell new initiatives. If you cannot sell, you cannot lead.

First, do not think only about what you are selling. You may be very excited about your idea. The bigger question is why should your listener be interested in your idea? Your enthusiasm for a new way of cleaning toilets may enthuse you, but not everyone is necessarily excited about toilet cleaning. So you have to get into their shoes and get into their heads and see the world through their eyes. You have to start not with your idea, but with their problem.

Everyone is selling: ideas, proposals and social events. We normally sell at three levels:

■ features ('My computer has 1024k memory');
■ benefits ('It can handle video editing');
■ dreams ('It could turn me into a Hollywood mogul').

Features are about the product and rarely appeal to anyone except geeks. Features are things like engine size, and the alphabet soup of technical specs for your computer.

Benefits are unique to each person and are more compelling. These are things like 'Daz washes whiter' and 'This car goes faster/is safer.'

But if you can tap into people's dreams then you are winning. These are things like:

■ 'You will look cool and successful in this car/jacket/etc.'
■ 'Presentation training will help you with your amateur dramatics skills and ambitions.'

■ 'This diet/facelift/botox makes you look young and sexy.'

Avoid selling features. At least work out the benefits, or ideally the dreams, that will appeal to the person you are selling to. Start with what the person wants, not with what you have.

Exercise 2.5:
Selling features, benefits and dreams

Work out how to sell the following, using features, benefits and dreams. Then see which sounds most convincing:

■ a fridge, to a desert nomad, a local family and an Inuit;
■ an off-road car to a school mum, a farmer and a football star;
■ a pencil to an illiterate tribesman, a child and a cosmonaut.

> **If you can tap into people's dreams then you are winning.**

NOTES

_____

_____

_____

_____

_____

_____

_____

3.2 Selling: Tapping into people's minds

We have already met fear, greed, idleness and risk in motivation skills. We meet them again in selling skills. They work together:

■ *Fear:* What problem am I solving for the other person?
■ *Greed:* What hope or dream am I helping the other person achieve?
■ *Idleness and risk:* Am I making it easy for the other person to agree? Have I removed the risks he or she perceives?

Do not start with your product, idea or perspective. The other person does not care about it. The starting point is that person's hopes, fears, dreams and risks.

You can use this not just for selling Daz. You can use it for selling your project, your idea or your proposal to peers and bosses alike: tap into their natural fear, greed, idleness and risk aversion.

As a simple exercise, look at how you might use hopes, fears, idleness and risk to sell an off-road vehicle to a school run parent and to a business person. Now do the same exercise with selling a mobile phone. (See Table 2.3.) In both cases you will probably find:

■ Trying to focus on features such as engine size is not very compelling.
■ The selling proposition varies dramatically depending on who you are selling to. You succeed when you focus less on the product and more on the buyer's needs.
■ The way you convey the message is not the same as the message. The sales person will not say 'This car is for snobs' but will hint at the status associated with the car ('This is a limited edition version', 'Many people want it, but few can afford it', 'It seems to be very popular with rock stars/people with country estates/explorers' etc).

Table 2.3 Using hopes, fears, idleness and risk in selling

	Off-Road Vehicle (School Run Parent)	*Off-Road Vehicle (Business Person)*	*Mobile Phone*
Hopes – what the person wants	Show you are a caring parent – and be one up on other parents.	Look cool, affluent and adventurous – and look down on lesser mortals.	
Fears – what is the fear this might remove?	Safety for children.	Very safe in bad weather.	
Idleness – how do I make it easy for the person to buy and use?	We will fit child locks and seats for you.	No hassle: insurance and servicing included.	
Risk – how do I eliminate the perceived risk of purchase/use?	Your spouse will like it as well.	Other business people buy this (you will not look stupid in this car...)	

> **Do not start with your product, idea or perspective.**

NOTES

_____

_____

_____

_____

_____

3.3 Selling: The selling process

It is not enough to know what to sell. You also need to know how to sell. Below is a classic seven-step sales cycle:

1. Agree the problem/opportunity.
2. Preview the benefits of addressing the problem/opportunity.
3. Suggest the idea.
4. Explain how it works.
5. Pre-empt objections.
6. Reinforce the benefits.
7. Close.

Check reactions at each stage. The cycle can take from 30 seconds (suggesting a dinner date) to years (selling a fleet of aircraft). The most important step is the first: agree the problem/opportunity from the buyer's perspective. Until you know what the buyer wants/needs to buy, you do not know what you are selling.

Consider the example of suggesting a drink after a long day at work using the seven-step cycle:

1. 'It's been a hard day.'
2. 'We all need to relax.'
3. 'Let's go for a quick drink.'
4. 'The pub is next door.'
5. 'I'll buy the first round.'
6. 'We can all unwind there.'
7. 'Last person out, turn off the lights.'

When you start, this process can feel complicated. Get used to it and it soon becomes second nature. Ideally, the process is a conversation in which you let the other person talk. You simply use the process to check where you are in the conversation and where you want to guide it next.

There are two important exceptions to following this process. First, if the person is ready to agree with you, move straight to the close. At this stage, the more you say, the more you are giving the person the opportunity to rethink the decision and say no. Many sales have been lost by the seller getting overenthusiastic and carrying the conversation on for too long. Second, if you find the other person starting to make objections, you have three choices:

1. Respond to each objection. This is obvious, but highly dangerous. You may well find that, instead of helping the conversation, you land up in an increasingly bitter argument. The reason for this is that you may well not have understood the problem that you are solving for the other person, so the best course of action is often to;
2. Quietly go back to the start and make sure you understand the problem. This avoids an argument and gets you both back to agreeing with each other.
3. Finally, you may decide that the objections are not substantive: they may well be an emotional and automatic response. Do not respond rationally to such objections: it simply invites an argument. The great sales people find ways of ducking the objection completely by changing the subject, distracting the person or making a joke. The buyer rarely wants to repeat a half-baked objection, so will be happy to move on with you.

Exercise 2.6:
The sales process

Go back to the fridge, the car and the pencil from Exercise 2.5. Try selling them using the seven-step framework.

Until you know what the buyer wants/needs to buy, you do not know what you are selling.

NOTES

_____

_____

3.4 Selling: The art of the close

Buyers are not mind-readers. They do not know what you want them to do. You have to ask them: you have to close the discussion and the sale. This causes some sales people to panic. In reality, it is easy. The buyer is expecting you to ask for something; otherwise that person would be wasting his or her time talking to you. So make sure you ask and close.

When someone is ready to agree, let the person agree by closing the sale. Bank it. Do not go on selling: you may land up unselling by mistake.

There are four main ways of closing a sale/discussion:

1. *The alternative close:* 'Do you want the red car or would you prefer the blue car?' You are not offering the choice of no car. Sneaky and effective.
2. *The action close:* 'Here are the car keys. Just sign on the line and I will guide your new car out of the showroom.'
3. *The direct close:* 'Do you want to buy the car?' Very dangerous: the person might say 'no'.
4. *The assumed close:* 'So we are all agreed that we are buying a fleet of pink and yellow cars.' Often used by those chairing meetings.

Exercise 2.7: Closing

Try all four types of close for the car and the mobile phone from Section 3.2.

Note down each time you are in a meeting how effectively people close and what lines they use. Start building your own list of effective closes.

If a close fails, look back and see what went wrong:

■ Check against fear, greed, idleness and risk.

- Check against features, hopes and dreams.
- Check against the seven-step sales process.
- Check against the close.

Buyers are not mind-readers.

The buyer is expecting you to ask for something.

NOTES

_____

_____

_____

_____

_____

_____

_____

_____

_____

_____

_____

_____

_____

3.5 Selling: The ultimate secret

Great leaders and great sales people share a common secret: they have two ears and one mouth.

> ### Exercise 2.8:
> ### Have you got what it takes?
>
> Count the number of ears and mouths you have. You may well share the secret of leaders and salespeople.

But the ultimate secret is that great leaders and salespeople not only have two ears and one mouth: they use them in that proportion. They listen at least twice as much as they talk. You will be surprised at how often managers talk themselves into submission, buyers talk themselves into buying and lovers talk themselves into bed. Let people listen to their favourite voice, their own, and they will think that you are wonderful.

Listening skills are covered in Part 4, Section 5. Once you can really listen, understand and learn, you are on the path to success. You may think that listening is just a sneaky sales trick. It *is* a sneaky sales trick. But it is also much more than that. When you are in a meeting with senior people, observe closely who does the most talking. It is normally the more junior people, who are pitching their ideas to the more senior people, who do all the talking. The senior people, like judges in a courtroom, have all the power and need to ask a little and say even less. Talking less and listening more is the privilege of power.

Exercise 2.9:
Listening

Try it.
A few hints to help you reflect on an important discussion:

■ Who was asking more questions? If you were focused on answers, not questions, you were probably talking more than listening.
■ Write down how much you learned from the other person: if you have fully understood the other person's hopes, fears and dreams you were probably listening well.
■ Ask a neutral third party who he or she thought was doing the talking versus the listening.

Leaders and salespeople not only have two ears and one mouth: they use them in that proportion.

Let people listen to their favourite voice, their own.

NOTES

_____

_____

_____

_____

_____

_____

Section 4
Coaching

4.1 Coaching: Purpose

The art of coaching is about helping people discover their own potential and resolve their own issues. It is not about telling them what to do or solving all their problems for them.

As a coach, you have a range of possible actions:

■ instructing, telling and solving problems;
■ giving advice and guidance, and suggesting ideas;
■ giving feedback to people;
■ asking questions to understand the context;
■ looking for options;
■ listening, summarizing and reflecting.

The basic idea is to gravitate towards the bottom of the list.

For a coach, solving problems for people is a fatal mistake. It is attractive because:

■ You get to look smart.
■ The other person is happy because you have made life easy for him or her.
■ You become more popular.

In the short term, this is attractive. In the longer term it is the road to ruin because:

■ The more you solve problems for people, the more they will bring their problems to you. You will land up with the problems of the world on your shoulders.
■ You are not letting your staff develop: the only way they will grow is if they climb their own mountains. You can guide, support and encourage them. But you cannot climb the mountain for them.

Gravitating towards the bottom of the list is hard work. Listening, summarizing and reflecting take time. And it is extremely frustrating when you know the answer, and your team member is struggling to find it. You may develop blood blisters on your tongue from trying to avoid blurting out the answer. But the time invested in helping the other person discover the answer pays big dividends. You can help people become better team players so that they can start taking problems from you, rather than bringing problems to you.

There is one risk of coaching and letting your team members come up with a solution: they may come up with a better solution than the one you had thought of. Fortunately, the coaching method means that you will not have exposed your half-baked idea to them. Instead you can nod sagely at their great idea and let them proceed. As the leader, you take responsibility for the success or failure of the team, so letting them come up with the smart ideas is 100 per cent in your interests.

Focus on asking open questions (see Part 4, Section 5). These are questions to which a yes/no answer is not possible: open questions encourage people to talk.

Exercise 2.10: Coaching

A colleague and friend from another department seeks your advice. You know she has been looking unhappy. Now she says she has been offered another job at a competitor. She asks you: 'In my shoes, would you take the job?' What are the questions you would ask to help her make her own mind up?

The more you solve problems for people, the more they will bring their problems to you.

NOTES

_____

_____

_____

_____

_____

_____

_____

_____

_____

_____

_____

_____

_____

_____

_____

_____

_____

_____

_____

_____

_____

_____

_____

_____

_____

_____

4.2 Coaching: Structure

A good coaching session has a structure. Typically there are four steps:

1. *Agree the goal/purpose of the session:*
   - 'What do you want to focus on/achieve/review today?'
2. *Understand the context:*
   - 'Why is this important to you now?'
   - 'What is the situation?'
   - 'How do the other people see the situation?'
   - 'How do you know that?'
   - 'What do you/others feel about the situation?'
   - 'What are the potential consequences of this?'
3. *Create and evaluate options:*
   - 'Have you seen anything similar before? What happened?'
   - 'What choices do you have? What do others want?'
   - 'What are the risks and benefits of each course of action?'
4. *Conclude:*
   - 'So tell me what you are going to do next.'
   - 'Will anything prevent you doing this?'
   - 'Do you need any help or support?'

Notice that each element of the structure is based around open questions, not on giving answers. Besides giving answers, the other core technique is silence, often referred to as 'wait time'.

Wait time is very difficult to achieve. Many people feel uncomfortable with silence. But do not feel obliged to fill the atmosphere with your brilliance. You need to give space for the other person to think and reflect, especially the more introverted types who like to think before they speak. Give them time, and the quality of discussion will rise.

Exercise 2.11:
Coaching structure

Use the questions you have developed in Exercise 2.10 and the structure in this section to role-play the exercise outlined in

Exercise 2.10 with a colleague. Alternatively, create your own role plays. Using the colleague/friend from another department, the possibilities might include:

- ■ 'I think my boss is fiddling expenses. Do I tell Accounts?'
- ■ 'One member of my team is making no effort at all. I have tried everything. But he seems to have the confidence of my boss. What can I do?'
- ■ 'My head of department insists I must go to a presentation next week. It is the day of my child's school play, which I missed last year. I had booked holiday. What can I do?'

Many people feel uncomfortable with silence. But do not feel obliged to fill the atmosphere with your brilliance.

NOTES

_____

_____

_____

_____

_____

_____

_____

_____

_____

_____

Section 5
Managing expectations

5.1 Managing expectations: Upwards

Expectations management is the lifeblood of corporate failure and success. There are three versions of the expectations game:

1. *The boss game*
   The boss wants to set the toughest expectations possible. If you can deliver against high expectations, that eases pressure on the boss to deliver in other areas.
2. *The team game*
   The team wants to have the lowest possible goals, so that they can be achieved with the minimum of effort and risk.
3. *The handover game*
   A departing manager will bequeath to the incoming manager a rosy picture of imminent success. If the incoming manager accepts this, he or she is dead meat: success will be put down to the work of the departing manager, and failure will be because the incoming manager is incompetent. Consequently, the incoming manager will rewrite history fast to paint a picture of imminent catastrophe. In this version of reality, the incoming manager cannot lose: if disaster strikes then it was the fault of the departing manager. If success happens, it is because of the heroism of the incoming manager.

This is not a game just for politicking middle managers. Look at how often profit warnings follow the appointment of a new CEO: the new CEO then makes a series of exceptional charges and write-offs to correct the failings of the previous CEO.

This is not always an uplifting game to play, but it is essential to survival. There are two golden rules to playing it well: play it hard and play it fast:

■ *Play it hard.*

Anchor the debate around the most extreme case you can justify, and then marshal as much hard evidence as you can to justify your position. You will be negotiated down from the extreme position: this will show flexibility on your part while still enabling you to chase a reasonable goal.

■ *Play it fast.*

Set expectations as early as you can. The later you leave things, the harder it becomes to change. If a top-down planning assumption of 20 per cent growth is made, you will find it hard to anchor the discussion around zero growth. If you have been in a post for two months, everyone will assume you will deliver on the targets your predecessor left you. Challenge and change expectations early.

> **Set expectations as early as you can.**

> **Challenge and change expectations early.**

Idleness and success: a case example

Paul was about the idlest person in the office. But he always got the best bonus, and all the top management thought he was a great leader and produced wonderful results. He only seemed to work really hard for about one month a year. This was deeply irritating to the rest of us who worked hard all year for a lot less money and even less praise.

The one month Paul really worked hard was during the budget cycle. He would start setting expectations very early in the cycle. He would show how his part of the marketplace was falling off a cliff edge in terms of customer demand; he would prove that the competition was investing heavily. He would prophesy, Cassandra-like, the imminent collapse of civilization, or more specifically of profits. He would play hardball over this and overwhelm people with data to show he was right.

By the end of the budget cycle, he would be committed to a very low profit target. He would also have secured a large increase in resources to fight off the competition. He would then, heroically and against all the apparent odds, overachieve against the profit goal (even although it was lower than the previous year's goal). For this great achievement, he would get a great bonus. The rest of us, who had boldly accepted the stretching and challenging targets that management wanted to impose, would struggle all year to hit target and achieve a modest bonus.

NOTES

5.2 Managing expectations: Downwards

Managing expectations downwards is nearly the mirror image of managing upwards expectations. An effective leader needs to be unreasonable, selectively. In setting expectations, the leader learns to be selectively deaf: you will not hear all the excuses about rising input costs, increasing competition and demanding customers. You will stretch the team as far as it can go. This is important because people tend to rise or fall to the level of expectations set for them.

In schools, the power of expectations setting is well established: expect kids to succeed and they will do well. Expect them to fail and they will fulfil your expectations completely. In this respect, business people are like schoolchildren: they rise or fall to the standard expected.

Effective expectations management is not only about setting expectations at the right level. It is also about setting the right psychological contract between the leader and the team member. The psychological contract has various elements on the leader's side and on the team member's side.

The leader's side of the contract is:

■ Deliver bonus and promotion promises if performance justi-fies it.
■ Give political support for dealing with other departments.
■ Be clear about what working style works best in the team.
■ Demonstrate an interest in and commitment to the future of each team member.
■ Delegate effectively: give interesting opportunities, not just administrivia.
■ Provide appropriate coaching.

The team member's side of the contract is:

■ Deliver the results promised.
■ Be 100 per cent loyal to and supportive of the leader.

■ Work in an appropriate style for the current leader and team.
■ Avoid surprises.
■ Don't whine and undermine the morale of the team.

Within these very broad expectations there is a huge amount to be discussed. What are the right goals? What is the right working style? What is the best mix of assignments? Leaders cannot expect their team members to be telepathic: it helps to set these expectations explicitly. The expectations need to be discussed, not mandated. If team members feel involved in agreeing and setting expectations, they are much more likely to feel committed to them than to arbitrary expectations set from on high. Expectations setting should always be a two-way process.

> **An effective leader needs to be unreasonable, selectively.**

NOTES

_____

_____

_____

_____

_____

_____

_____

_____

_____

_____

Section 6
Managing upwards

6.1 Managing upwards: Principles

Even the CEO has to report to the chairman. Managing upwards is part of being a leader. The easy thing to do is to whine about the boss. Many of us have good cause to whine about past or present bosses. But whining does not make for a good leader. As leaders, we need to take control of our destiny, however abysmal our boss may be.

Here are four principles for managing the boss well:

1. Deliver the results: manage the psychological contract.
2. Adapt your style.
3. Manage your context.
4. Manage yourself: avoid the SAD syndrome.

Deliver the results: manage the psychological contract

The psychological contract with your boss is more important than the employment contract with your firm, until your boss tries to fire you... This normally is based on the same formula, with many variations: you deliver the right results at the right time in the right (the boss's) way, and the boss delivers the right assignments, bonus and promotion. If either party fails to deliver on its side of the bargain, then a divorce normally follows.

To manage the psychological contract, you also need to manage expectations. You are unlikely to work on an assembly line where your output can be measured and compared by the week, day, hour and minute. You are likely to live in a world of ambiguity and uncertainty. The boss does not really know how much you can do by when. Most bosses adopt a simple rule: they keep on piling up the work until they can no longer ignore your shrieks of pain. You need to be very clear about what you can do and when you can do it. It is better to have a difficult conversation early on than it is to suffer days and weeks of agony failing to deliver impossible results against an impossible deadline.

If you deliver results and manage expectations, you are 80 per cent of the way to success.

Adapt your style

Styles of management were covered in Part 2, Section 2. The relationship with the boss is unequal: you are less important to the boss than the boss is to you. The boss can fire you; you cannot fire the boss. From this truism, the reality that follows is that you are the one who is going to have to adapt your style: do not expect the boss to adapt to you.

Manage your context

Dysfunctional bosses enjoy master-slave relationships. Your slavery will be complete if you have not managed your context well. You need to find other senior allies, coaches and supporters in the organization. Make yourself useful to senior people. Volunteer for stuff: they will appreciate the help. Ask for their advice: they will be flattered that you trust them. As you find a few sponsors, these are the people who can help you. They can provide advice on how to deal with an awkward boss; they may even coach the awkward boss directly. They are also your emergency escape hatch: when things get tough they can find you another boss, even themselves, so that you can escape your master-slave relationship.

Manage yourself: avoid the SAD syndrome

A poor boss will create the SAD syndrome: stress, anxiety, anger and depression. These are not good qualities for a leader. They lead to poor performance and bad interactions with people, which will make relations with the boss even worse. This is a vicious circle. The only way out is normally out of the organization. This achieves nothing. When you leave, you help the boss look good even if you give a damning exit interview. The boss simply observes that you were not performing and that, as your exit interview shows, you were always complaining and sapping team morale. So the boss took the tough decision to 'let you go'. The boss is now a hero, and you are a zero.

Dysfunctional bosses enjoy master-slave relationships.

The psychological contract with your boss is more important than the employment contract with your firm.

NOTES

_____

_____

_____

_____

_____

_____

_____

_____

_____

_____

_____

_____

_____

_____

6.2 Managing upwards: Cardinal sins

There are almost an infinite number of ways to upset a boss. I was able to watch four security guards remove a marketing director from his office: one took hold of each limb and carried him out of the front door. His sin? He always walked through doors in front of the CEO, which made the CEO feel he was being upstaged. Foibles and egomania aside, our research found a few common cardinal sins that bosses find difficult to forgive:

- ■ disloyalty;
- ■ surprises;
- ■ outshining, outflanking or outsmarting bosses;
- ■ not delivering: reliability;
- ■ unprofessionalism.

Disloyalty

Disloyalty is by far the most unforgivable sin. Even the most demanding bosses tolerate occasional mistakes, bad jokes, bad dress and even bad performance. But disloyalty breaks the fundamental psychological contract between the boss and the team. Disloyalty is not just about bad-mouthing the boss. It is also about failing to support the boss and the team in a tight corner or failing to speak up when it is needed. If the team is to succeed, each team member must know that he or she can trust and depend on every other team member. When times are tough is when trust is most needed and is either built or lost fast.

Surprises

Bosses don't like surprises. Don't hide bad news. Deal with it early; set expectations well.

Outshining, outflanking or outsmarting bosses

Like you, your boss needs and wants to look good. Many bosses also have fragile egos. Do not try to steal their thunder. Help them. Good bosses will give you plenty of chances to shine.

Not delivering: reliability

Sometimes there are no easy short cuts. Ultimately, you have to deliver, even if it is hard work.

Unprofessionalism

This covers a multitude of sins. Keep careful note of the behaviour that pleases or annoys the boss. It can be small things like timeliness, who walks through doors first, who speaks up at meetings and when, dress codes, use or non-use of humour and more.

Disloyalty is by far the most unforgivable sin.

NOTES

_____

_____

_____

_____

_____

_____

_____

_____

Part 3

Moment of truth skills

Section 1
Learning to say no

1.1 Learning to say no: The art of buying time

This is a critical skill for any leader. The art is to say no without appearing negative.

In practice, saying no is tough because very often you are ambushed by an idea and you are put in a position where you feel the need to respond yes or no. The first principle comes from the need to avoid the commitment ambush by buying time.

The art of buying time

When you are asked to take something on, go along with a new idea or support some initiative, you need time to think. You can buy time by asking questions. At all costs, avoid giving answers. The temptation may be to curry favour by going along with an idea for a while. You will then find yourself quickly committed to a course of action that you will slowly regret.

Go back to the coaching principles in Part 2, Section 4 to work out how to ask questions that will sound constructive. The goal is to ask open questions and follow the coaching model:

1. *Agree the goal of the idea:*
   - What is the problem this idea solves? For whom?
   - What are the benefits of doing this? For whom?
2. *Understand the context:*
   - Who is sponsoring this?
   - What are the time frames?
   - What support and resources will be available?
   - Why are we looking at this now?
   - How does this fit with our other priorities?

3. *Create and evaluate options:*
   - How else can this be achieved?
   - What are the obstacles to success?
4. *Conclude:*
   - What are the next steps?

By the time you have gone through the first three sections, time will have elapsed to let you think and you will have gathered enough information to make an informed decision about what you want to do. You may even want to say yes instead of no. It is also possible that the other person will have talked him- or herself out of the original idea and into another, better idea.

As a leader you will be coming up with ideas you want others to agree to. Now turn the exercise above on its head: work out what all your answers to the questions above will be. You may convince yourself you need a better idea: at least you will have saved yourself the embarrassment of suggesting a half-baked idea. But if you can answer all the questions clearly, then you probably have a good idea and are well placed for a discussion with others about it.

At all costs, avoid giving answers.

NOTES

_____

_____

_____

_____

_____

_____

_____

1.2 Learning to say no: The cheese shop game: 'no' with no 'no'

Leaders know 'no' is a no-no in corporate life. Saying no makes you look negative and not action-focused. But occasionally you need to stop insanity happening. You have been through the coaching method of reviewing an idea, and still the idea is floating around like a bee with a bad attitude and a big sting. You need to do something to get rid of it. Welcome to the cheese shop game.

The cheese shop game

The cheese shop game was devised by Monty Python. A shopper enters the cheese shop and asks for a named cheese like Stilton or Cheddar. The shop owner has to find a way of saying that he has not got that cheese without saying he has not got it. Excuses might be things like:

■ 'Sorry, out of season...'
■ 'Haven't you heard about the health scare?'
■ 'Right out of fashion.'
■ 'I wouldn't sell that to my dog.'

The person who first runs out of cheeses to name or excuses loses.

The corporate cheese shop game

In the corporate version of the cheese shop game, you have to find reasons for resisting an idea without saying no to the idea. There are three main routes of defence for you:

1. *Priorities:*
   – 'How does this fit with my other priorities? Which ones would you like me to defer for this idea?'
   – 'Should we do this before or after X episode (which is more urgent/on the critical path)?'
2. *Process:*
   – 'Could we do it this other way instead?' (Better, faster, cheaper, less risky.)

- 'How can we set this up for success?' (People, budget, time: connects to priorities.) Make the conditions for success so large that the others give up the idea.
- 'Why don't we do a full evaluation/test of this first to de-risk the idea?' By the time the evaluation is done, everyone will have moved on to the next bright idea anyway.

3. *People:*
   - 'Who is this for?' (Connects to priorities.) If it is not for a powerful sponsor, question whether the idea can really succeed: urge the others to get a better sponsor, which they may find impossible.
   - 'Who is best to do this (not me)?'

Beyond the cheese shop

The ultimate form of resistance is to do nothing. Do not argue with or oppose the idea. Let other people take the heat for you. Only fight the battles you really have to fight. By doing nothing you create the one enemy that most corporates cannot defeat: inertia. There are so many other things going on that no one can find the time and energy to make the idea you dislike gain momentum. If the idea does gain momentum despite you doing nothing, you have plenty of opportunity to leap on board the bandwagon as it slowly trundles into motion.

Leaders know 'no' is a no-no.

The ultimate form of resistance is to do nothing.

NOTES

_____

_____

_____

_____

_____

_____

_____

_____

_____

_____

_____

_____

_____

_____

_____

_____

_____

_____

_____

_____

_____

_____

_____

_____

_____

Section 2
Conflict management

2.1 Conflict management: Principles

Organizations are set up for conflict. This is a surprise to most people, who think that organizations are meant to be as cooperative as bees in a beehive. So let's emphasize the point: *Organizations are set up for conflict.*

Different functions, business units and geographies will have different priorities. Internal conflict, be it nice or nasty, is how these conflicting priorities are resolved. Conflict is good, provided it is contained. Unconstrained conflict and open warfare are not good. The question is how leaders deal with the conflict when it arises.

From this simple observation comes the first principle of conflict management: do not take it personally, especially when it is meant to be personal. If you sink into the gutter in personal battles it does not matter if you win or lose: you will still smell awful. Stay aloof from the gutter and at worst you will get your ankles splattered. This is easy to say but hard to do. We need a simple tool that we can deploy in a conflict emergency. Welcome to turning the FEAR of conflict into the EAR of consensus.

Let's start with nasty conflict that feels highly personalized. The natural reaction is fight or flight: punching the CEO or running away is not good tactics. But the fear is real: we have to deal with it. Take the F out of FEAR (the bad response) and you are left with EAR (the good response).

FEAR stands for:

Fight furiously.

Engage the enemy emotionally.

Argue against all-comers.

Retaliate, and repudiate reason.

This can be fun, especially on your final day at work. It is also very common and very unproductive: it invites an intellectual, political and emotional punch-up.

EAR stands for

Empathize.

Agree the problem.

Resolve the way forward.

In the heat of battle, this is much harder and much more productive.

> **Organizations are set up for conflict.**

NOTES

_____

_____

_____

_____

_____

_____

_____

_____

_____

_____

_____

2.2 Conflict management: Practice

So how do you put your EAR into practice?

Empathize

Do not hug the other person. This might be misunderstood. Listen past the bluster and blame. Listen past the emotion. Let the person talk. Listen actively to show that you understand. Look at the listening skills in Part 4, Section 5.

Let the person blow off steam and cool down. Make sure you really understand his or her situation. Do not try to put your own point of view forward or justify yourself: it will only cause more conflict. Do not try to fight emotions with logic. Don't enter the other person's personal space: step back and give him or her time to cool off.

Agree the problem

Try to focus on the actions, outcomes and benefits desired. Do not do this until both of you are breathing normally and not shouting. When have you had sustained success from shouting at other people? This is where you move from listening and paraphrasing to asking questions:

■ 'So what we need to achieve is...?'
■ 'So where do we need to get to by next week/month?'
■ 'What does the customer want as a solution?'

Resolve the way forward

Curiously, this is often the easiest part. Once you have all calmed down and agreed the situation and the problem, then the way forward is often clear, if painful. To help resolve the way forward:

■ Generate options: do not get stuck with a single-point solution.
■ Get the other person to suggest more than one idea.

■ Formally agree the next steps: ask the other person to summarize and then confirm the way ahead in writing.

Exercise 3.1:
Practising conflict management

Set up a role play with a tolerant colleague. Try getting really angry and shouting at your colleague. As a courtesy, let the colleague do the same to you. In both cases the 'victim' should just empathize. See which of you can sustain the anger longer. You will find it takes a huge amount of energy to sustain anger. It is emotionally draining. Anger pretty quickly blows itself out if it is met with the damp sponge of empathy.

As a second exercise, see what happens if the 'victim' starts to retaliate. Do not do this for too long, because emotions can get pretty high. Anger feeds on anger: soon you will both be in a shouting match.

It takes a huge amount of energy to sustain anger.

NOTES

_____

_____

_____

_____

_____

_____

_____

2.3 Conflict management: Tips of the trade

Beyond theory, there is reality. Below are some of the most common conflict management tips we hear suggested in workshops:

1. *Become a fly on the wall.*
   Observe yourself: your language and your body. The fundamentalists of this out-of-body approach to conflict call for Zen-like detachment. You do not have time to go to a monastery to master meditation. So, in the short term, pretend you are a (smart) fly on the wall. Observe the emotion of the other person, but do not respond or get caught up in it. Imagine that it is a game: the goal is to manipulate the other person into calmness and agreement. It is easier to play a game where you know the rules than it is to fight a battle where you do not know the outcome.

2. *Detach: how would someone else handle this?*
   We all have role models who do things very smoothly. Imagine you are your role model. What would he or she do next? How?

3. *Escape to a happy land.*
   Everyone has a happy land in their heads to which they can escape at moments of idleness or stress. Go there. Chill out. Some people play games in their happy land where they can see the other person as a baby, or dressed in a tutu, or being wiped out by a machine gun firing rotten eggs. It is quite difficult to get angry with a fat 50-year-old whom you see dressed in a tutu or as a baby throwing toys out of the pram.

4. *Depersonalize: blame the situation, not the person.*
   When battles get personal, they get nasty. Instead of blaming someone for messing up, look at the context and circumstances that led to disaster. Perhaps there was not enough time or support, or lack of clarity around expectations. There are many reasons why things go wrong. Once you start this discussion, you defuse the emotion. You can start to deal with reality.

5. *Buy time: it is hard to sustain anger.*
   If you follow the FEAR to EAR principles you will be buying time. As we have seen, it is tough to sustain anger. Let it vent. Then you can deal with reality.

It is quite difficult to get angry with a fat 50-year-old whom you see dressed in a tutu or as a baby throwing toys out of the pram.

NOTES

_____

_____

_____

_____

_____

_____

_____

_____

_____

_____

_____

_____

_____

_____

_____

2.4 Conflict management: A radical alternative

Just occasionally, it is possible that we do something wrong. In many organizations, the standard operating procedure at this point is:

1. Deny any wrongdoing: it has all been misinterpreted; that is not what happened.
2. Spread the blame: you were told to do it or you were let down by someone else.
3. Change the subject: in a superior way point out that we really should be focusing on more important issues, unless of course everyone wants to play the blame game...
4. Shoot the messenger: this is mischievous gossip by rivals and others who are, as usual, up to no good and poisoning the well of corporate well-being.

Under extreme circumstances, try a radical alternative: apologize. This needs courage and strength that few people have, and it needs to be done right.

The power of 'sorry'

If you know you are in the wrong, it can be highly effective and unusual to say 'sorry', which is a word that hardly exists in the corporate language. Be aware that when people are angry they are incapable of listening. You will often need to repeat the apology several times: this can be incredibly frustrating because it feels like people are rejecting you and your big gesture. In truth, they may not be able to listen past their emotions. Also, they will be picking up far more cues from your body language and tone of voice than from what you say. So if you start jabbing your finger at them and shouting 'Look, I've said sorry five times! Get it?' do not be surprised if their anger rises.

You will also need to act fast. Get your apology in early: the longer things are left to fester, the worse they become. People take positions, stories become exaggerated and a molehill becomes a mountain. Snuff the fire out before it spreads.

A sorry knight's tale

He had a knighthood, and he was very proud of it. He could bore for Britain on any subject, and he did. He thought a knighthood gave him the equivalent of papal infallibility.

In retrospect I was, perhaps, being marginally undiplomatic when I told him he was being arrogant and narrow-minded. The knight of the realm promptly exploded with pompous rage.

At this point, I was at decision time. I could deal with either reason or emotion. Dealing with reason I could have shown why I felt he was being arrogant and narrow-minded. But fighting emotion with reason is like fighting fire with petrol: it is not a smart idea. You have to fight emotion with emotion. We could deal with reality and reason another time. So I decided to say sorry. I had to say it eight times before he even heard it. This was painful. I felt like shouting at him for being so stupid and not listening and for ignoring my gesture of apology. I felt like giving him another sort of gesture altogether. But I kept calm, and then he calmed down.

He slowly realized he had now been arrogant, narrow-minded and pompous while making a fool of himself in public. He spent the rest of the day apologizing to me. So I would then apologize to him (again) and everything was sweetness and light.

Saying sorry is never easy. But say it early, keep saying it, keep your cool and even the most pompous and cloth-eared knight will get the message. Of course, the real message should be to avoid getting into situations like that in the first place. But life would then be very tedious. And sometimes it pays to stand up to people (see Part 3, Sections 4 and 7).

Under extreme circumstances, try a radical alternative: apologize.

Fighting emotion with reason is like fighting fire with petrol.

NOTES

_____

_____

_____

_____

_____

_____

_____

_____

_____

_____

_____

_____

_____

_____

_____

_____

_____

_____

_____

_____

_____

Section 3
Crisis management

It can't happen to us. Disasters are what happen to other people. Muggings, murders and mayhem belong to a different world from our nice, rational and safe world. And then it happens, and you are the leader. It's 2.30 am and you are at a conference in the wrong time zone. A panic phone call wakes you up in your hotel room. What should we do? The press are on to us; the board want to know what is happening; friends and relatives are clamouring for information; everything is moving fast. Is the situation under control? Hell, no – that's why we called you: you're the leader. Tell us what we do – now.

This is what the textbooks euphemistically call a 'moment of truth'. You are about to be made or broken by what happens next.

Crisis management does not start with the crisis. It starts long before. Recognise that it is not a question about if a crisis will happen, but what, where, who, when and why it will happen.

There is a three-part way of dealing with crises:

1. prevention;
2. preparation and practice;
3. prompt, professional, positive and proactive response.

Prevention

The best way to handle a crisis is to prevent it. Do a risk audit with your team. What are all the things that can go wrong? Work out the major categories:

■ *legal:* employment, discrimination, product liability, confidentiality;
■ *criminal:* fraud, theft, terrorism, violence, denial-of-service attack;
■ *health and safety:* working practices, product contamination and scares;

- *technical:* data loss, power loss, water loss, website or IT systems crash;
- *operational:* loss of service, production, key staff;
- *financial:* bank covenants, takeover threat, receivables;
- *market:* loss of key contracts, customers, suppliers.

Find out what the major crises have been in the rest of the organization and in your peer group organizations. This may mean that, like old generals, you find you are preparing to fight the last war. But it also means you are preparing against the most common and likely risks.

Preparation and practice

Prepare to respond not only to the known risks (above) but also to unknown and unplanned risks. You will not have time to prepare when the unexpected happens: you need to have a few preconditioned responses that will at least buy you enough time until you can regain control of the situation. The preparation typically focuses on:

- *Decision-making clarity.* Be clear who has authority for releasing emergency spending and communicating to the media, staff, owners and customers.
- *Communications.* How will everyone communicate with each other? How will you find them in the middle of the night when no one is at the office? Who are the key people who need to come together to manage any crises: legal, PR, technical, HR etc?

Take a little time to practise. Every organization does fire drills, although fire is one of the less likely disasters to strike. Prepare for other disasters as well: the whole of London's financial district goes through regular disaster recovery exercises. If a city can do it, so can an organization.

Prompt, professional, positive and proactive response

The Hitch Hiker's Guide to the Galaxy had a very simple motto: 'Don't panic.' That could also be the motto for dealing with crises. This is difficult to do under stress and when everyone else is in a panic. But there are some common themes to handling crises from the minor to the major:

■ *Prompt response*
A fast response is needed to provide reassurance that everything is being done to solve the crisis as fast as possible. This neutral response is about buying time while finding out what is really happening and regaining control. In the first stages of a crisis, emotional reassurance is as important as a logical response. This may not buy much time, but it helps.

■ *Professional response*
People will judge you by how you appear and act as much as by what you say. If you appear calm, collected and committed, they will respond better than if you look in a panic.

■ *Positive response*
The leader needs to avoid letting the organization get into buck passing and playing the blame game. Make the team focus on discovering what they can do collectively to regain control and move forward. In the process of doing this, they are also likely to find out the root cause of what went wrong: it is hard to regain control without knowing why control was lost in the first place. But you can leave the inquests for later.

■ *Proactive response*
Your task is to come up with the plan as fast as possible. The plan will inevitably change as events unfold. This is unimportant: as long as people have some sort of plan to work for, they can make progress. Morale will rise simply by virtue of feeling that there is direction, there is a possible solution and they are making progress. If 50 per cent of the initial effort is wasted because the plan was not perfect, then be happy that 50 per cent of the effort was making a difference. As things become clearer, so you can focus and refine the effort.

> **Don't panic.**

NOTES

_____

_____

_____

_____

_____

_____

_____

_____

_____

_____

_____

_____

_____

_____

_____

_____

_____

_____

_____

_____

_____

Section 4
Dealing with bullies

It is very fashionable, in a postmodernist way, to avoid criticizing personal styles of management. It may be fashionable and post-modern, but it is also wrong. Here we will look at just two examples of destructive leadership styles: aggressive and passive.

Aggressive leaders fancy themselves as superheroes. The conference circuit and bookshops are full of these superhero stories. Aggressive superheroes think that only they can save the day because everyone else is too lazy or stupid. The results are:

■ a demoralized organization, which many people leave;
■ no effective succession, because the leader has not given anyone the opportunity to grow: this leads to failure when the leader leaves, proving to the leader that he or she was the only person saving the ship from disaster;
■ a high dependency on the success or failure of one individual: in the United States, quite a few heroes are now in the tender care of the district attorney.

Passive people are unlikely to become leaders, unless daddy owns the firm. They set themselves and the organization up for failure. Although they are not to be found at the tops of organizations, there are plenty of passive people lower in the organization. As leaders, we have to work with both passive and aggressive types of person.

The ideal way forward is assertive leadership: this is positive, professional and proactive. It enables everyone to win, not just one person. (See Table 3.1.)

The essence of the assertive leadership style is:

■ Be clear about your agenda and needs.
■ Explain, not tell; persuade, not order.
■ Understand and respect others' needs.

Table 3.1 Personal styles

	Passive	*Assertive*	*Aggressive*
Characteristics	Allow others to choose for you; inhibited; set up to lose.	Choose for self; honest; self-respecting; win/win.	Choose for others; tactless; self-enhancing; play to win.
Your Own Feelings	Anxious, ignored, manipulated.	Confident, self-respecting; goal-focused.	Superior, deprecatory, controlling.
How You Make Others Feel	Guilty or superior; frustrated with you.	Valued and respected.	Humiliated and resentful.
How You Are Seen	Lack of respect; do not know where you stand.	Respect; know where you stand.	Vengeful, fearful, angry, distrustful.
Outcome	Lose at your expense.	Negotiated win/win.	You win at others' expense.

■ Balance active listening with talking.

■ Set up win/win outcomes, not win/lose.

Against an aggressive bully it takes nerve to maintain the assertive style. Success depends on:

■ *Preparation*
Know exactly what your interests are. Most of the time you can avoid a fight either by conceding things that are not important to you or by doing a judo throw: finding a way of aligning your interests with the bully's so that you work together, not against each other.

■ *Professionalism*
Do not rise to the bait and fight: the bully will enjoy that far too much. If you fight, the bully will have to be seen to win

and make you be seen to lose; otherwise the bully's self-perception will be destroyed. It will be a nasty fight, and the bully has far more experience of fighting like that than you do.

■ *Practice*
Once you get used to it, dealing with bullies becomes a game to enjoy. You can observe their antics with a level of detachment and respond appropriately. Bullies know when they are wasting their time: they will go in search of an easier victim.

With a passive person the challenge is reversed. Instead of needing to take heat and energy out of the system, the assertive leader needs to inject some heat and energy into the system. This goes back to the fundamental motivation skills in Part 2, Section 2, which look at how you can find the triggers that will activate each individual.

Aggressive superheroes think that only they can save the day because everyone else is too lazy or stupid.

NOTES

_____

_____

_____

_____

_____

_____

_____

_____

_____

Section 5
Negative feedback

5.1 Negative feedback: The SPIN model

No one likes giving or receiving negative feedback. But not telling someone he or she is failing to meet expectations perpetuates the problem, misleads the individual and will create a crisis of trust and performance later. So deal with it promptly and give the person a way forward.

SPIN is a classic and simple framework for giving feedback:

- *S: Situation and specifics*
  Give feedback in the right situation: when the person is calm and the event is still fresh in the mind. Do not give feedback when people are angry, stressed, upset or very busy. When you give feedback, be specific about your purpose (why are you doing this?) and the circumstances and the event.
- *P: Personal impact*
  Do not judge the other person: that invites conflict. Tell the person how his or her actions made you feel: feelings are irrefutable. For example, say 'You have turned up late to three client meetings: it makes me feel you think they are unimportant' not 'You are a lazy idler', or 'I was very embarrassed when the CFO saw the errors in the budget you prepared' not 'You are an innumerate scumbag.'
- *I: Insight and inquiry*
  Ask questions to see if the person understands the problem, to help him or her explore and evaluate options and to discover the way forward. Avoid telling people: make them learn for themselves.
- *N: Next steps*
  Mutually agree what happens next. There needs to be a positive way forward. You need to have thought through possible options and actions. But, at this point, it is often better to go into coaching mode (see Part 2, Section 4) and get the person

to generate the options and the way forward. The person may come up with a better and more relevant solution than yours. In any event, people will feel more committed to their solutions than they will to yours.

Get the person to summarize the next steps. This is the best way to check for understanding: people can only summarize well if they have heard and understood well. The act of summarizing will also help people consolidate their own thinking and they will remember the feedback much better and, it is to be hoped, positively. Follow up in writing to confirm the understanding.

No one likes giving or receiving negative feedback.

NOTES

_____

_____

_____

_____

_____

_____

_____

_____

_____

_____

_____

5.2 Negative feedback: SPIN in practice

Giving negative feedback is like coaching. It is about helping other people discover for themselves what they need to do. Like coaching, it is about asking the right sorts of questions.

It is also important to adopt the right style. Table 3.2 gives a few pointers to success and failure.

Table 3.2 Finding the right style

Success	*Failure*
Specific feedback	Generalized feedback
Balance positive/negative comments	All negative
Actionable	Non-actionable
Deal with the problem	Attack the person
Asking, involving	Telling
Understand the situation	No understanding

Ultimately, there is little point in giving negative feedback unless you can drive to action. Once you have validated the problem, you need to find some way of resolving it. The feedback session will be much more positive and productive if it is couched in the language of 'development', 'finding a way forward' or 'putting in place the skills and behaviours required for success'. Each person will have language they prefer. It is best to find actionable, future-focused and positive language. Backward-looking and analytical language ('Let's see how you messed up') rarely helps.

Exercise 3.2:
Giving negative feedback

Try any of these role plays with a trusted colleague. Before starting each role play, think about the following:

■ How will you apply the SPIN model?
■ What are the specifics you have observed and how have they affected you?
■ What are the open questions you will ask?
■ What are the next steps you would want to see?

Role plays:

■ A client has complained that one of your team members has been late on delivering key reports twice.
■ Some of your team members are complaining that another team member is too negative and drains morale and energy.
■ A high-flying team member is suddenly not delivering to the standard or timing you expect.

Help other people discover for themselves what they need to do.

NOTES

_____

_____

_____

_____

_____

Section 6
Hearing feedback

6.1 Hearing feedback: Discovering the truth

In most cultures, bosses do not like giving feedback, especially if it is negative feedback. Like the jilted spouse who is the last to discover the truth, so the last person to hear about a performance problem is the owner of the problem.

In theory, you should be able to ask for feedback and you should get it. In theory, wars, famine and poverty should not happen. In practice, you need three other strategies for finding out where you stand:

1. *Watch the feet, not the mouth: actions speak louder than words.*
   You will know how well you are doing by how far your boss entrusts more work, and more important work, to you. If you are being overloaded with highly demanding work, do not complain too loudly: this is a sign that the boss trusts you personally and values your ability to deliver results. If you find yourself with time to burn while all your colleagues are very busy, start to worry. Start asking for assignments: if you are met with evasive answers and prevarication then that is a sure sign the boss is not confident about you. You need to start finding some simple tasks where you can deliver, demonstrate your competence and build trust.
2. *Listen to the silence.*
   You know what the formal evaluation criteria are for your role. You should also understand the informal evaluation criteria your boss will use. Listen carefully to any comments your boss makes and see which criteria he or she is talking about. Then listen very carefully indeed to what the boss is not saying. If the boss praises you on five criteria and ignores another four, you should ask yourself (and your boss) why there is such silence on the missing topics. At best, the boss

simply has no information about those areas: make sure you provide the boss with the evidence required. It may also be that the boss has some concerns. Find out about them early and you can do something about them.

3. *Be your own boss.*

Evaluate yourself against three key benchmarks:
 – How am I doing against the formal evaluation criteria?
 – How am I doing against the informal evaluation criteria?
 – How am I doing against the best of my peer group?

This is how the boss will think. If you have already thought this through you will at least be well prepared for the evaluation meeting with your boss. More to the point, you will be able to take action to make sure you are performing well.

> **The last person to hear about a performance problem is the owner of the problem.**

NOTES

_____

_____

_____

_____

_____

_____

_____

_____

_____

_____

_____

6.2 Hearing feedback: Listening through the pain barrier

When you are hearing feedback, it is very easy to hear badly. The three most common mistakes are:

1. *Dr Pangloss's trap*
   Voltaire's Dr Pangloss declared that 'Everything is for the best in the best of all possible worlds.' We like to hear good news, and at least some of us have cloth ears when it comes to bad news. The shrinks say that we are in denial. It can be painful to hear bad news, but it is important to hear it so that we can act on it.

2. *The Cassandra trap*
   Cassandra did not actually say that 'Everything is for the worst in the worst of all possible worlds', but she was still a pretty miserable companion. She was always foretelling doom and gloom. Sunny weather would, for Cassandra, simply be a prelude to a storm. Just as some people cannot hear bad news, so others only have to hear a marginally adverse comment to go into paroxysms of despair. You need to hear both: build on strengths and find ways of working round weaknesses. Some bosses advise you to 'work on your weaknesses'. This is a recipe for disaster: no one succeeded by working on weaknesses. Like sports people, leaders do not focus on weakness: they focus on their strengths.

3. *The perceptions trap*
   Perceptions may not be real. But the consequences of perceptions are real. The boss may be wrong to think that you are an idle layabout. The perception may be wrong, but the consequences of that perception will be very real.

When you are hearing bad news do not get defensive or aggressive. Try to listen objectively. Go back to some of the principles of coaching (Part 2, Section 4) and giving feedback (Part 3, Section 5). Make sure that you understand what is being said and then how you can jointly move to action:

1. What is the issue we are talking about?
2. What are the practical and specific examples of this issue? Is this an occasional and minor matter, or a regular and serious matter?
3. What are some alternative strategies for dealing with the examples raised? How would the boss have dealt with those situations differently?
4. How can we move forward?
   - What coaching and training support is available?
   - What does this say about the sorts of assignments I should take on?
   - What are the practical next steps?
   - When shall we meet again to review progress?

Make sure that you leave with a positive, and shared, agenda about how you will work together on the topics identified. Give the boss some stake in the game, through a coaching, training or assignment responsibility. And then follow up: make it impossible emotionally, politically or rationally to return to the same negative issues at the next formal review meeting.

Perceptions may not be real. But the consequences of perceptions are real.

NOTES

_____

_____

_____

_____

_____

Section 7
Fighting battles

The enemy within is often more deadly than the enemy at the gates. The competition might be laying siege, but at least they are still outside the town walls. Your colleagues have the means, the motive and the opportunity to slip the knife between your shoulder blades.

Sometimes, fighting is unavoidable. But take care. Sun Tzu in *The Art of War* advocated fighting under only three conditions, all of which must be present: 1) Only fight when there is a prize worth fighting for. 2) Only fight when you know you will win. 3) Only fight when there is no alternative.

1. *Only fight when there is a prize worth fighting for.*
    Too many corporate battles are fought over trivia. If there is a trivial battle being fought, step aside and let others cover themselves in mud. If necessary, be noble and make a concession. You will now have earned some credit, and someone will owe you a favour.
2. *Only fight when you know you will win.*
    On Wall Street, if you don't know who the fall guy is, you are. If you must fight, win. A dead hero is still dead. All battles are won and lost before the opening shot is fired: make sure you have the political support and ammunition to win before fighting.
3. *Only fight when there is no alternative.*
    It is better to win a friend than it is to win an argument. If you win an argument and make an enemy, the enemy will still remember you long after the argument has been forgotten.

Inevitably, there is an alternative strategy, which was advocated by Lord Nelson in his many battles against France and its allies: 'Any captain of mine who lays his ship alongside that of the enemy can do no wrong.' This ultra-aggressive doctrine would, on occasion, have small British ships attacking French battleships. The French knew they would have to fight if they went to sea, so they stayed in port where their fighting capabilities deteriorated fast.

The Nelson doctrine is much used by entrepreneurs and a breed of self-styled hero leaders. When it works, it is highly effective and the leader is destined for the cover of *Fortune* magazine. For every successful hero leader, there are the corpses of thousands of dead would-be heroes.

It's your life; you decide.

The enemy within is often more deadly than the enemy at the gates.

If you don't know who the fall guy is, you are.

It is better to win a friend than it is to win an argument.

NOTES

_____

_____

_____

_____

_____

_____

_____

_____

_____

Section 8
Managing adversity

Sometimes things can look very bleak indeed. All leaders have crises: even Churchill had his 'wilderness years' between the wars. That came to a 20-year stretch of adversity.

There are typically five stages of dealing with major adversity. These were identified by Elisabeth Kübler-Ross in her research on the process of dying (*On Death and Dying*, Touchstone, New York, 1969). They are often seen as the stages people go through in dealing with any major setback in life:

1. *Denial:* 'I can't be on the slippery slope (of real or corporate life). I'm a winner.'
2. *Anger:* 'Why me? It's not my fault. I don't deserve this.'
3. *Bargaining:* 'Is there a way out? If I do x or y, can I buy some time?'
4. *Depression:* Reality sets in, but in the gloom there seems to be no way forward.
5. *Acceptance:* 'I accept my fate and am ready to move on to another life.' At least in corporate life, this is where the leader takes control and starts the process of renewal: death in one corporate life is the prelude to rebirth in another life of leading in the corporate, public, voluntary or entrepreneurial worlds.

It helps to recognize these symptoms. If you feel them you are not abnormal: you are a human being suffering the normal reaction to loss and adversity.

From a leader's perspective, these are unhelpful reactions. Inaction, depression and seeking to blame people are not recipes for success or recovery. To recover you need to focus on the future:

■ *Create some options.*
   Find some ways to success or recovery, in your current environment or another one.
■ *Take control; be proactive.*
   Do not wait for others to control your destiny for you.

■ *Find some balance.*
Your current employer does not own your soul. Know what is
important to you and focus on making that work.

Do not read Nietzsche; that will only make your adversity feel
worse. But do remember the one useful thing he said: 'That which
does not kill you makes you stronger.' Most leaders learn from
experience and from adversity. Surviving adversity builds knowledge and resilience.

Exercise 3.3:
Reviewing adversity

Review a big setback you have had:

■ How did it feel against the five-stages framework?
■ How did you handle each stage?
■ How could you have handled it better?

Keep this in mind next time you face a major setback: preparation makes you stronger.

To recover you need to focus on the future.

NOTES

_____

_____

_____

_____

Part 4

Technical skills

Section 1
Reading

Of course, we all know how to read, write, talk and listen. Don't we? It's just that our colleagues write drivel, never listen properly, don't read our elegant prose and bore us to tears with their presentations. We are all each other's colleagues...

Reading socially is different from reading for business. Reading socially, we want to have our heads filled with surprise, delight or shock with what we are reading. Reading for business we do not want our heads randomly filled with what the writer writes. We need to read with prejudice, to read with an agenda of our own so that we are not sidetracked by the internal logic and brilliance of the document in front of us.

Reading socially, we let the writer stay in control and lead us. Reading for business, the reader needs to stay in control. Being led by the writer is a recipe for being led astray.

Exercise 4.1:
Reading (and meeting) with intent

Before reading a significant business document, take a moment to note down the following three things:

1. *What is my point of view on the subject being discussed?*
   This helps you avoid being caught by its internal logic. With an established point of view, you will be able to dazzle your colleagues with perspectives that they had not thought about, because they had let themselves get caught by the internal logic of the paper in front of them.
2. *What topics do I expect to be covered?*
   This helps you spot the invisible: things that have been omitted. You can also think of this as 'What questions would I want to ask and have answered?' You will now look brilliant as you spot the invisible: the gaps that the writers hoped you would not notice.

3. *What actions or coaching items do I want to pursue with the writers when I see them?*
    This allows you to create a proactive agenda rather than being caught in the writers' agenda. You will now appear like a wonderful, sage-like coach who is positive, constructive and helpful.

This exercise can also be applied to meetings. With practice, you will become very good at it. You will be in danger of looking insightful and proactive: you will always seem to come up with insights, spot omissions and drive to action. It comes down to learning to read: read with prejudice, with an agenda and with preparation.

Reading socially is different from reading for business.

NOTES

_____

_____

_____

_____

_____

_____

_____

_____

Section 2
Writing

We can't all be Shakespeare, and we don't need to be. But we do need to be effective in how we write. The best editor I ever had beat five writing rules into me. I still fail, but at least I try...

1. *Write for the reader.*

    Who are you writing for and why? Ask yourself why the reader should want to read your document and what you expect the reader to do as a result of it. This is your critical first step from which you can decide the purpose of the document, its storyline and the critical content. If you are unclear for whom you are writing, you are likely to land up with an unclear document.

    Where you are writing for a group of people, work out which ones are essential to you. There will be one or two critical decision makers whom you need to influence: focus your document on them rather than trying to please everyone. A focused document will be much more powerful than an amoeba-style document that lacks shape, direction, backbone or purpose.

2. *Tell a story.*

    What is the one headline you want the reader to remember? Construct a storyline to support the headline. Throw away all the verbiage that does not drive to the headline. This helps you achieve clarity and focus. Do not start with all the facts and data you have lovingly assembled at great personal effort and cost. Start by asking:

    - What is the message I need to get across? One message is enough: two only confuses people for whom your document is one of several hundred they will see during the week. The message is driven by whom you are writing for (see above).
    - What is the minimum amount of information required to support the message? What other information directly supports the message? All the other information can disappear into a nice fat appendix, which everyone will ignore,

but it will reassure them that you have done lots of work.

Even if you are simply writing a regular report, this is still an opportunity to tell a story about what is happening in your business and what needs to happen next. Every document should have a purpose, and the purpose should be communicated through a story. Long after the data have been forgotten, the story will be remembered - if you have bothered to work out what the storyline is.

3. *Keep it simple.*

Use short words and short sentences. Remember the ditty: 'When writing, keep it short: A dozen words at most per thought.' Writing short is far harder than writing long. As Churchill noted at the end of a long letter to his wife: 'I am sorry I wrote you such a long letter. I did not have time to write a short one.' If you have a clear storyline, you should be able to keep it short.

4. *Make it active.*

The passive and impersonal do not make a document look businesslike: they make the document boring. Make it readable instead, if you want it to be read.

5. *Support assertions with facts.*

If something is important, urgent or strategic, explain why it is important, urgent or strategic to your reader. Otherwise you invite the reader to argue: 'It may be important to you, but it's not to me.' And take care: one bad fact will make the reader distrust everything you write.

Exercise 4.2: Writing to be read

Take the longest PowerPoint presentation you can find and reduce it to one headline of 10 words maximum. Then draft a story of up to 100 words for it. Then draft a new six-page PowerPoint presentation. See if the short or the long version has more impact.

We can't all be Shakespeare, and we don't need to be.

NOTES

_____

_____

_____

_____

_____

_____

_____

_____

_____

_____

_____

_____

_____

_____

_____

_____

_____

_____

_____

_____

_____

_____

Section 3
Presenting

3.1 Presenting: Substance

We have all sat through tedious presentations where the presenter fills the air with nothing more than self-importance and incoherence. Let us not inflict the same fate on others when we present.

A simple starting point for presenting is to work on the writing skills to establish the story and content you want to cover.

The ancient Greeks treated public speaking as an art form. For them, and for us, good speaking has three elements, logos, pathos and ethos:

■ *Logos or logic*
Good speakers quickly answer the question 'Why should I, the listener, listen?' They then say what they are going to say, say it and conclude by saying that they have said it. Clear, simple, effective and 100 per cent free of bad jokes badly told. The logos is essential in the first minute: you have to establish why they should want to listen. What is the problem, opportunity or perspective that they need to hear from you?

■ *Ethos*
This answers the question 'Why do I believe this person?' Build credibility fast; use facts to support assertions. Borrow credibility by quoting people who have helped or supported what you are doing.

■ *Pathos*
This builds the emotional connection with the audience. Facts and logic are not enough. Tell a story and relate your message to their needs and their experience.

Building ethos, pathos and logos depends on knowing who you are talking to. The larger the group, the more mixed it is. In this case, figure out whom you really want to influence. It is likely to be just one or two very important people. Focus your efforts on those people. It will make the entire presentation seem more focused and lively. It will also be more persuasive to the person or people you want to persuade.

Exercise 4.3:
Becoming a great Greek (and business) demagogue

Work out your logos, ethos and pathos for the following:

- Introduce your organization to an industry conference with 300 people present.
- Review what you have learned about leadership with a group of 20 at a company away day.

Logos, ethos and pathos.

NOTES

_____

_____

_____

_____

_____

_____

_____

3.2 Presenting: Style

Style counts. Over 70 per cent of the information we absorb is visual. So if you are the king of the mumblers, dress like a tramp and slouch like a teenager in full hormonal angst, the brilliance of your message will be lost on the audience. Instead, focus on the three Es:

- energy;
- enthusiasm;
- excitement.

Think of the worst presentation you have attended. Did it have the three above characteristics? Probably not.

Some practical tips to help you:

- *Throw away the script.*
  You will sound wooden. Instead, memorize your opening to make a good start. Memorize your conclusion to make a good finish. Memorize some choice phrases that you can insert on your way through: each phrase is a way marker on your speech. You will keep your structure and discipline while sounding spontaneous.
- *Avoid complicated slide presentations.*
  If you have slides, the principle is to have stupid slides but a smart presenter. The slide might have three or four key words to help the audience anchor where you are: you provide the commentary. The nightmare is to have smart slides that explain everything and a stupid presenter who reads the slides more slowly than the audience.
- *Stand on the front of your feet, so that a slip of paper could pass under your heel.*
  Weight on the back of the foot encourages slouching and down energy.
- *Engage the audience.*
  Look individuals in the eye, rather than gazing into the middle distance. Do not stare at one person the whole time. Get into a rhythm of using and completing one phrase or sentence

while you look at one person and then move on to the next phrase and the next person in another part of the room. This has three valuable effects:

- The audience will be electrified and pay attention when they all know they are likely to be engaged directly by you. Put the other way: if you appear to ignore them, do not be surprised that they appear to ignore you.
- You stay very aware of how people are responding to you.
- Your own energy levels will go up, you will appear very focused and the audience will respond with high energy and focus.

■ *Rehearse.*

The more you rehearse the more confident and comfortable you will feel. Even if you cannot rehearse everything, make sure you do the following minimum rehearsal:

- Rehearse the first 30 seconds intensely. When you start is when your nerves will be highest and everything can come out all wrong. But if you are word-perfect in the first 30 seconds, then you will make a smooth and confident start, the audience will engage with you and you will have time to settle down.
- Rehearse the key phrases you want to use to make key points and to move from one part of the logic flow to the next. Work on the choice phrases: people will remember them long after they have forgotten everything else.
- Rehearse the last 30 seconds. 'Are there any questions?' is a feeble finish. Effective finishes often include a direct appeal to the audience, such as 'I wish you all success on this great adventure we are now starting', 'I look forward to working with each one of you on this exciting initiative' or 'Each one of us can now leave a lasting legacy.'

The three Es are greatly enhanced by two more Es: expertise and enjoyment. If you are expert at your subject, you are more likely to relax and enjoy what you are saying. If you are enjoying it, your audience is likely to enjoy it as well. If you hate it, do not expect the audience to enjoy it.

Exercise 4.4:
Presenting

1. Try telling someone about how the cost allocation system in your organization works. See if you fall asleep before your audience does.
2. Now try recounting one of the most memorable events in your career. You will naturally display all five Es: energy, enthusiasm, excitement, expertise and enjoyment. Such a simple exercise shows that we can all speak well: we simply have to transfer our skills on to the big stage.

Have stupid slides but a smart presenter, not the opposite.

NOTES

_____

_____

_____

_____

_____

_____

_____

_____

_____

_____

_____

_____

Section 4
Storytelling

Try this simple exercise:

1. Recall and explain a spreadsheet from a month ago.
2. Recall and give an account of a memo or e-mail from a month ago.
3. Recall and retell a story you heard from a month ago.

Normally, this exercise works. Do not, however, try it with a group of actuaries: you will spend the next three hours being told about spreadsheet, disasters and triumphs. But back on Planet Earth, most earthlings find it far easier to recall a story than it is to recall a spreadsheet or a memo. Presentations will be recalled only if they told a story, not for the brilliant words and numbers that the presenter slaved over for days and weeks.

Leaders understand the power of a story. A good story is memorable and has emotional intensity that no amount of facts and argument can achieve. Most corporate stories talk about the journey we are taking, and the obstacles and opportunities that lie along the road. Effective leaders are often effective storytellers.

A good story has the following elements:

■ Meaning and relevance to the listeners or readers: remember you are writing for the readers, not for yourself.
■ A storyline, which will have:
  – A beginning, which is often framed as a challenge for the hero or organization to overcome. The resolution should not be clear from the start, as otherwise all the suspense and interest are lost.
  – A journey, which tells how the challenge was or will be overcome.
  – An ending: a resolution in which there is often a lesson or a sudden insight or reversal of fortune. The best stories have an element of suspense and uncertainty.

■ Emotional impact: readers or listeners should be able to see themselves in the story, and should be able to see themselves overcoming the challenge presented.
■ Authenticity:
  – The story should come from your heart so that it has your voice and your passion behind it.
  – The story should relate to a reality that both storyteller and listeners recognize.

To see the power of stories in action, look at the stories chairmen and CEOs spin to the financial media. They tend to be captured in a few very simple headlines:

■ 'We are entering a price war, so we are going to cut costs hard.'
■ 'We need scale economies to drive down costs, so we will acquire other companies and integrate them.'
■ 'No one is competing in the bottom end of the market, so we will enter it.'
■ 'We will diversify our sources of income into less cyclical markets.'
■ 'We are going to refocus on a few core businesses where we are leaders, and sell the other businesses.'

Each of these simplistic headlines may reflect months of work, and may well drive the efforts of the whole organization to success or failure. But they are very simple messages that most people can remember easily and act on.

Ivan's terrible day

Ivan was in despair. He had tried everything to show that a major change in strategy was required. He had charts and data and research in plenty of reports and PowerPoint presentations. The more he hammered away at his facts and figures, the more things went wrong: some people would nitpick his data; others would simply switch off under the barrage of data. In his frustration he went to the flip chart and drew a picture.

'Look,' he said, 'we are on this side of the river. We are being attacked non-stop by competitors who are taking our territory. On the other side of the river there are these green pastures that no one has yet occupied. And the good news is there is the bridge to those green pastures if we can work with the right partners. We need to move now, before it is too late.'

There was a deafening silence. People looked at the picture. It might be possible to argue with some of the detailed numbers. But everyone knew in their hearts you could not argue against the big picture. The reality was staring them in the face: they knew they had to move. The meeting switched gear from analysis and denial to working out how to move across the bridge. From then onwards, crossing the bridge to the green pastures became part of the language of the organization.

Exercise 4.5:
Telling the story of your journey

Develop a story that tells about the journey that you are taking your organization on. Work out how the story changes for your team members, for other departments and for the CEO. It helps to think about:

■ What do they need to know about the journey?
■ What might their role in the journey be?

Develop a story that talks about the journey you are on: are you on the right journey, or do you need to turn down another road?

A good story is memorable and has emotional intensity that no amount of facts and argument can achieve.

NOTES

_____

_____

_____

_____

_____

_____

_____

_____

_____

_____

_____

_____

_____

_____

_____

_____

_____

_____

_____

_____

_____

_____

_____

_____

_____

_____

Section 5
Listening

Listening is the leader's secret weapon. It is easy to tell people what to do, how to improve or how to solve their problem. Instead of telling, try asking and listening. Let them discover what to do and how to improve. Let them discover the answer to their problem. That way they have more ownership and commitment to the way forward, and they learn some skills and independence in the process.

There are three keys to effective listening:

1. *Paraphrasing*
   When someone talks, try paraphrasing back to them what they said. If you get it right, the other person will be delighted that you were listening so well. If you get it wrong, you will quickly avoid any future misunderstandings. Paraphrasing is not the same as agreeing: it simply shows you have understood the other person.
2. *Asking open questions*
   The more open the question, the more people talk. A closed question gets a yes or no answer. It gives little information and often leads to conflict. Open questions often start 'How would you...?', 'Why did they...?' or 'What would you do if...?' Closed questions often start 'Do you agree...?' or 'Shall we...?'
3. *Debriefing*
   After any significant meeting, spend a few minutes debriefing with a colleague. You will both have heard and seen different things. Together, you will quickly get more intelligence and feedback than if you try scribbling notes furiously during the meeting. An effective debrief will cover the following:
   - *Hot buttons:* What were the hot buttons for each person at the meeting? Did we press the hot buttons effectively and get people properly engaged around their issues? Did everyone have the same hot button or different ones?

- *Red issues:* What were some of the objections, issues and challenges people raised against what we were saying? Did we handle them? What do we do about them next?
- *Roles:* Who had what role in the meeting? Who is the real decision maker? Do they all have a common agenda or not?
- *Body language:* What was that telling us about how people were feeling about each of the topics that arose?
- *Our own performance:* How did we do? What could we do better both individually and as a team? How can we divide up responsibilities better next time?
- *Next steps:* What happens next and who is going to do it?

Listening judo

Chris is an expert at listening judo. He always has very strong opinions and he likes to get his way. He does so not by talking, but by listening. He is so smart that he knows the best thing to do is to shut up and listen at the start of a meeting.

When everyone has had their say, and largely cancelled each other out with their contradictory views, Chris will step in to offer a summary of what he has heard. He will then carefully extract a few half-formed ideas that he has heard from each person. He will present them back to the group as the wonderful ideas that Kate, Julia, Jim and Amir had. As he does this, you can see Kate, Julia, Jim and Amir puff up with pride. Each person's idea has not only been heard in the babble of the meeting: it has been recognized as a smart idea and it is seen as that person's idea. Everyone is now eating out of Chris's hands. No one is going to argue against him, because that would be tantamount to arguing against their own ideas.

Naturally, Chris's summary just happens to support the prejudiced agenda that he entered the room with. By the end of his summary, the war is over. Chris has not only won the intellectual battle, but he has won friends all around the room.

Long after the meeting is over, Chris will still attribute all the great ideas not to himself but to others. As a result, he builds networks of deeply loyal colleagues and there is no chance that the ideas are going to get unpicked.

Exercise 4.6:
Listening skills

1. Try paraphrasing, perhaps in a role play with a colleague. After your colleague has spoken, summarize by saying 'So what you mean is...' or 'If I can summarize what you said...'
2. Create a list of open and closed questions you can ask in different situations. Start by noting what sorts of questions other people ask and whether those questions get productive or unproductive answers.
3. Test your listening skills by doing debriefs with a colleague who has been to the same meeting as you. Ask the following:
   - Who said what? (Who was in favour? Why? Who was against? Why?)
   - How did people react at different stages (body language as well as words)?
   - What did you learn about the agendas and priorities of each person present at the meeting?
4. Video yourself and focus on questioning. Make a T chart. On one side, keep track of the number of open questions you ask. On the other, keep track of the closed questions. What sorts of responses do these elicit?

Listening is the leader's secret weapon.

NOTES

_____

_____

_____

Section 6
Doing numbers

Managers use numbers the way drunks use lamp posts: for support, not illumination. We all know what the answer should be in the bottom right-hand corner of the spreadsheet. So we manipulate the assumptions until the correct number appears, with a bit of safety margin thrown in for good measure.

For the leader, reviewing a spreadsheet is not about the numbers: it is about the assumptions that lie behind the numbers. An effective leader has three ways of testing the numbers:

1. *Know your key data inside out.*
   You lead the business: you should know the key numbers and ratios. Do not get confused by the whole spreadsheet: look at the key numbers and ratios used and see if they fit with what you expected. If not, push hard to find out why.
2. *Play that 'What if…?' game.*
   You should know not just the key numbers and ratios, but all the key sensitivities in the business. They might be prices, market share, market growth, costs, interest rates or many other items. Ask what assumptions they have made and how the result would change if different assumptions were made on these sensitivities.
3. *Know who is presenting the numbers and why.*
   The credibility of the numbers is directly related to the credibility of the presenter. A cautious profit projection from an executive with a great track record is worth far more than an exciting profit projection from an untested executive. Turn this logic around for a moment: if you are the presenter, make sure you have credibility on your side. Get the support of the finance department and of seasoned and trusted executives before finally presenting your numbers.

The leader also needs to beware of the motives behind the numbers. When not using numbers like drunks using lamp posts, executives will use numbers like lawyers using facts. They will use the numbers selectively to make a point. To see how far wrong this can go, look up www.countkostov.blogspot.com, which carries profiles of some of the worst abuses of numbers by apparently trustworthy bodies like charities, government, research groups and scientists.

Exercise 4.7:
The numbers (and assumptions) game

1. On a blank sheet of paper write down the key numbers and ratios for your business: financial, market and people numbers. Now compare them with the actual numbers. Draw up your key data list of the sacred and serious numbers and ratios you need. Learn them.

2. Play the numbers game. Look at a company budget or five-year plan: what are the key assumptions and how would you plausibly massage them to produce a huge profit or loss? What actions can you take to influence a positive outcome on the key assumptions?

Managers use numbers the way drunks use lamp posts: for support, not illumination.

NOTES

_____

_____

_____

_____

_____

_____

Section 7
Problem solving

7.1 Problem solving: Answering the right question

The first rule of problem solving is: do not try to do it all by yourself. A solo answer is rarely better than the group answer. Even if it is a good solution, no one else will own it and you will have to spend excessive time getting others to accept your solution. Let them work on the problem with you and own the solution with you.

As a leader you will not, however, simply present other people with a problem. You will have thought it through sufficiently to know:

■ You have the right problem.
■ You are focused on causes, not symptoms.
■ You know who need to be involved in the solution because of their skills, interest or position in the organization.
■ You have created some thought-through options.
■ You have a structure or approach for solving the problem.

The critical step is to find the right problem. Three questions for you to ask about the stated problem are:

■ Who owns this problem? Who really wants this fixed?
■ What are the consequences of not fixing it?
■ What are the consequences of solving the problem?

If there are compelling answers to these questions, you probably have the right problem and you will quickly find out who are the right people to involve in solving the problem.

Exercise 4.8:
Making sure you are solving the right problem

There are many good exercises to show how group problem solving is better than individual: go to www.wilderdom.com/games/descriptions/SurvivalScenarios.html for a selection of exercises.

Look at your current projects and see how well they fare against the three questions below:

- Who owns this problem? Who really wants this fixed?
- What are the consequences of not fixing it?
- What are the consequences of solving the problem?

Find the right problem.

NOTES

_____

_____

_____

_____

_____

_____

_____

_____

_____

7.2 Problem solving: Process and techniques

Welcome to the world of fish bones, six thinking hats, brainstorming, synectics, SWOT, Pareto analysis, decision trees, metaplanning, mapping, Chicago rules, concept fans and many more problem-solving techniques. There are countless problem-solving resources available on the web, and many facilitators if you need them.

The basics of any problem-solving process are relatively straightforward:

1. *Understand the problem.*
   Be clear who has the problem and the consequences of fixing it or not. Learn enough about the problem to know that you are focused on causes, not symptoms. Keeping asking 'Why...?' to find out the root cause of the problem.
2. *Create hypotheses.*
   Some people advocate complete brainstorming ('What if we covered New York with sticky treacle?'). But if you have really understood the problem, the answer is often not far away. To create insight as opposed to funky ideas, look at the problem from new angles. How do our customers see this? How will the competition exploit this? How has this been handled elsewhere in the world or in other industries?
3. *Evaluate and select the best hypotheses.*
   Don't waste time evaluating every option. Let the group pick the two or three they most want to work on. The best ideas normally come through. If you are leading the group, you can use leader's rights to add one more for group consideration.
4. *Drill down to action planning.*
   If the first three steps have been completed well, this is the easiest step. The drill-down may reveal further, lesser, problems, which can be solved with the same four-step process.

Facilitation techniques

Here are some simple rules to follow in a brainstorming, problem-solving and team-building meeting. You should ask a facilitator to enforce the rules. Like a referee at a sports game, the facilitator must avoid taking sides. The facilitator's job is to enforce the rules. Some facilitators have a long rule book of rules, which just gets in the way of a productive discussion. At most, you need four rules. People can just about remember and respect four rules. No one will remember a rule book with 50 rules, and you cannot follow what you cannot remember. The four rules are:

■ *Benefits before concerns*
   Smart people like to show they are smart by showing they have analysed a problem and found its weaknesses. This is good survival strategy: we avoid doing stupid things. But it also means that we kill ideas before we know how good they are. It is far tougher, and more productive, to understand the benefits of an idea before we see the concerns.
■ *No heat-seeking missiles*
   This is an extreme version of 'benefits before concerns'. Watch when an idea is shot down by a smart intellectual missile. Everyone quickly learns that having ideas is dangerous, so they shut up and that is the end of constructive thinking.
■ *Headlines before the detail*
   Think of newspapers: a three- or four-word headline is all you need to understand the thrust of a story. Stop people giving long speeches: focus on getting ideas out. This makes the facilitator's job easier: it is possible to write headlines on a flip chart; it is not advisable to try writing speeches on a flip chart.
■ *Express concerns positively*
   Instead of 'That's stupid: it costs far too much', try 'How can we improve the cost/benefit profile?' The first statement leads to conflict; the second leads to a productive discussion.

Like a good air traffic controller, a good facilitator will make sure that all the ideas that are raised land safely on the flip chart. When lots of ideas are flying, the facilitator will need to put some in a holding pattern until cleared for landing. A good facilitator will make this feel natural and productive to the group.

Exercise 4.9:
Using the problem-solving process

Use this framework to discuss with a colleague any of:

- How would you reduce crime?
- How would you increase pensions?
- How would you increase savings?
- How would you beat the competition?

You cannot follow what you cannot remember.

NOTES

_____

_____

_____

_____

_____

_____

_____

Section 8
Decision making

In theory, decision making is rational. Anyone who has been in an organization and been capable of fogging a mirror knows that this is not true.

Leaders always have to make decisions in a fog of uncertainty. In practice, they need ways to make the decision-making process easier. There are typically three foundations that leaders use to make decisions: rational short cuts, emotional interests and politics.

Rational short cuts

The most common short cuts in business are:

■ *Habit*
If something has worked before, do it again. If it ain't broke, don't fix it. These are risk-minimizing strategies that are attractive relative to taking on a new, unproven and potentially risky alternative.
■ *Credibility*
Look at the credibility of the person presenting the idea. Executives are often buying into the person as much as they are buying into the idea.
■ *Anchoring*
Debate is normally fixed around the first data point. For instance, in the annual budget round, the most bitter arguments are often at the end of the round and focus on relatively small line items. Meanwhile, the big battles are often missed completely at the start of the cycle when the planning assumptions were made. A planning assumption of 20 per cent growth and an assumption of zero growth lead to very different sorts of discussions.

The implications for leaders are clear:

■ *Habit*
Pitch a decision in a familiar framework as a low-risk continuation or extension of how things have been done before.
■ *Credibility*
Line up credible supporters to back your idea.
■ *Anchoring*
'Get your retaliation in first' is the motto of many contact sports teams. The leader needs to get in early and set the terms of the debate correctly from the start.

Emotional interests

Executives assess ideas from a personal impact perspective: 'How will this affect my workload, priorities, bonus and promotion prospects, and assignments?' Smart leaders will work the emotional agendas of each key decision maker one by one. These issues will not come out in any public forum overtly. Instead, an emotional problem ('This increases my workload too much') will find expression in a series of rational objections (cost, risk, value etc). The result can be disaster: there is an increasingly fractious debate about rational issues that are irrelevant. Once people have taken a rational position in public, they find it politically impossible to retreat. So they raise more and more rational objections that have nothing to do with the real source of their resistance.

An effective leader will work out all the emotional and personal challenges in private and in advance of any formal decision-making meeting. For the purposes of this sort of conversation, any meeting with more than two people in it is a public meeting.

Politics

Every part of an organization has different interests and different priorities. Leaders need to be sensitive to three sorts of political interest:

■ *Process*
Due process is important. For instance, the finance department may expect to be consulted on all financial numbers. If they are not consulted, do not be surprised to find them attacking your numbers furiously when they find them. Politically, they have to show to the organization that it is not worth trying to bypass them.

■ *Control*
No department likes to surrender control and authority. For instance, recruiting belongs to HR, and advertising to marketing: who owns the advertising in the jobs marketplace?

■ *Priorities*
This classically comes down to budget, people and time. If there is a fixed pot of money and people, and only a limited amount of management time and focus, then the competition for that pot will be ferocious. In most organizations, the competition is not in the marketplace. The real competition is sitting at a desk near you. This is where the leader has to craft carefully a coalition of common interests, by showing how different agendas can support each other.

The real competition is sitting at a desk near you.

NOTES

_____

_____

_____

_____

_____

_____

Section 9
Negotiations

9.1 Negotiations: Principles

Negotiations are a fancy form of selling and decision making. They are often misrepresented as battles where one side wins and the other side loses. In practice, effective negotiations are based on two fundamental principles: 1) win/win; 2) focus on interests, not on positions.

The idea of negotiating is not to trick the other side. That lands up in a fight, which you might not win. Instead of competing, collaborate. All the greatest victories are won without a fight.

To succeed without fighting, find out what the other person wants to gain from the negotiation. The challenge is to think a little further than cost or price. Think through what are the person's interests, and focus the discussion on interests not on positions.

For example, a salary negotiation seems a classic win/lose argument. One side pays too much or the other receives too little. Working on interests shows a different perspective. The employer will want to retain talent. But there will be other interests as well: perhaps there is a new programme to be started or a challenging assignment to be undertaken. The employee is not interested only in money. The employee will be thinking about career development, work-life balance, assignments and risk and rewards in measurement and appraisal.

Based on this, there can be a productive discussion around what the employee really wants going forward: how to balance work-life commitments, how much extra work, responsibility and risk the employee wants to take on, what skills the employee can develop and how much support and investment he or she should get (like money for training courses or sabbaticals). Suddenly, money becomes just one variable in a much wider mix. Both sides can now find areas of give and take and come to an outcome in which both sides feel they have had a win.

In a good negotiation, the language changes from a me/you discussion to a we/us discussion. You should both be working together to achieve a common outcome, rather than fighting against each other.

Negotiating a partnership

The partnership should have been a marriage made in heaven. Hiro brought some great product to the table; Jayne had a great client list to whom she could sell. They were introduced to each other and success looked assured. Then it all went wrong. Hiro immediately focused on how much equity he should get for his product: he wanted over half because there would be nothing without him. Jayne wanted over half because Hiro would not be able to sell anything without her. We went back to basics.

What Hiro really wanted was money (of course, but that is different from equity), recognition for his achievements and the chance to create some more exciting products. He hated the idea of getting bogged down running a business. Jayne wanted to build a business with a portfolio of products and a real team supporting her. By looking at interests, the two sides realized they could work together happily: Jayne would sell Hiro's product, brand it under his name and give him an advance so that he could continue research work without the hassle of managing a business and a royalty so that he could get rich if things worked well. Jayne kept 100 per cent of the equity. Both sides were happy: they got what they wanted.

All the greatest victories are won without a fight.

NOTES

9.2 Negotiations: Process

By now you should be familiar with the sales process. Negotiations follow the same logical flow. The difference from selling is that you are working together to develop the logic; you are not simply pushing your own logic and solution. The process is:

1. *Agree the problem.*
   What is the common opportunity or challenge we can help each other with?
2. *Preview the benefits.*
   What are the positive outcomes for each of us? What are our interests, not just our positions?
3. *Suggest the idea.*
   In negotiations, you want to explore a range of ideas and possibilities: do not get locked into a single-point solution that invites a yes or no response. Create room for manoeuvre.
4. *Explain how it works.*
   Work this together so that both sides own the solution: if both sides feel they own the solution, both sides will feel committed to it.
5. *Pre-empt objections.*
   Work together to identify the potential pitfalls and how you will overcome them.
6. *Reinforce the benefits.*
   Keep your eyes on the prize: this is why you are working together. And be very clear about what each side needs to deliver to the other side.
7. *Close.*
   Work out exactly what the next steps and responsibilities are, and then follow up.

This is rarely a single discussion.

You are working together: you are not simply pushing your own solution.

NOTES

9.3 Negotiations: Networks

Naive negotiators negotiate with one individual, hoping that the person has all the power, authority, responsibility, time and good will to deliver the entire organization in support of what you are negotiating. Real life is not like that. Many negotiations depend on influencing a whole network. If you depend on one person, you can depend on failure. It is up to you to identify and manage that network. Typically, there are six main roles in a negotiating network. They are:

1. *Authorizer*
    This person has the final decision-making authority and budget. You may only see this person at the very start and end of the negotiations. Even if you are lucky enough to have this person as your main contact, the person will still need your help in managing the decision-making network in his or her own organization.

2. *User/proposer*
    This is often the person you will negotiate with on a day-to-day basis. This is the person with the immediate opportunity or problem, where you are part of the solution. Ideally, you will turn this person into your coach (see below) so that you are jointly working to get the organization to support you. You want the user to be working with you, not against you: that requires understanding and respecting the user's real interests in the negotiation.

3. *Technical buyers*
    These people must be satisfied that policies, standards and procedures are met. They are often in places like finance, HR, or health and safety. They cannot approve the negotiation, but they can hole it beneath the waterline. These people are often ignored, which makes them dangerous. But involve them early, and they are often very helpful in clearing the way for you.

4. *Key influencers*
    These people may not be obvious on any organization chart. They have informal influence, not formal authority, over decision making. It could involve executive coaches, non-execu-

tive directors or senior non-line managers whom everyone trusts. Hunt them down: their opinions often carry weight because they are seen to be above the day-to-day political fray.

5. *Gatekeepers*

Gatekeepers provide or deny access to key decision makers. Secretaries are an obvious example. A good relationship leads to diaries becoming available; poor relationships mean the diary remains shut. Be careful of the executive who promises to get you access to the CEO or other senior leaders. This is often a simple power play: ' Do what I want and I (may) get you access to the CEO.' You have just lost control, and the chances of gaining the access you want are still close to zero.

6. *Coaches*

These are people on your side who want to guide you through the decision-making jungle. There is always someone in the organization who will see value in what you are doing and will want you to succeed. The ideal is to turn everyone in the negotiating network into your coaches: they should see themselves as partnering with you, not negotiating with you. If you have properly understood their interests, they will normally be more than happy to help and support you.

Exercise 4.10:
Influencing a network

These networks apply not only to sales situations. Try to map out the decision-making network for:

■ a major project you are trying to push through;
■ how your next bonus and promotion will be determined.

Once you have mapped the decision-making network, take the next critical step and identify for each person:

■ What are their hot buttons: what will make them support me?

- What are their red issues: what concerns or limitations (time, money, power) do they have?
- What do I need to do next to bring them along?

Keep one page per person, where you can keep track of contact details and each meeting you had with the person and the next steps. You will keep a complete map telling where you are and where you need to go to bring your project, promotion, proposal or bonus to a successful conclusion.

If you depend on one person, you can depend on failure.

NOTES

_____

_____

_____

_____

_____

_____

_____

_____

_____

_____

_____

Section 10
Networking

10.1 Networking: Breaking the ice

Some people love it; others hate it. Either way, you will have many opportunities to build your network within and beyond your organization. Most people flunk the opportunity. Watch what happens at conferences: people speak to people they already know, through shared geography, function or status. Very few people actually use the opportunity to extend their networks: people prefer to stay in the comfort zone of familiar faces. Leading from the comfort zone is not the road to success.

Networking is essential. Over 70 per cent of jobs are found through networking, not through headhunters and formal advertisements. Your career may depend on your network. Within your organization, you depend on networks to secure support for your assignments and to find your way to the next great assignment or opportunity.

Preparation is important. Know to whom you want to talk and why. Have a list of topics where you might want help and support: this will help you spot opportunities in the course of the conference or networking event.

A simple networking approach can be summed up as another alliterative three Es, engage, enthuse and enquire:

1. *Engage.*
   Prepare some standard ice-breaking questions. Royalty uses 'And what precisely do you do?' Get people talking about their favourite subject: themselves. They will like you for this. As they talk about themselves, you will find hooks to catch them with.
2. *Enthuse.*
   Build rapport. See the trust equation in Part 4, Section 10.2. You need to look for common interests: this could be work interests, pastimes or people whom you both know. Although

enthusiasm is still a certifiable disease in the darker recesses of the Civil Service, the rest of humanity finds enthusiasm infectious (unless your enthusiasm is train spotting, in which case you have probably not put this book in your anorak to read on the station platform).

3. *Enquire.*

Find out what they are interested in, and where the common points of interest are. Do not try to negotiate a deal there and then: suggest that it might be worth getting together later to discuss the matter in more detail. Do not put them in a negotiating position: make sure you have built rapport and earned the right to follow up.

Next day, drop an e-mail saying thank you and following up on any promise made.

**Let people talk about their favourite subject:
themselves.**

NOTES

_____

_____

_____

_____

_____

_____

_____

_____

_____

10.2 Networking: Building trust

There is a difference between knowing many people and having an effective network. An old-fashioned Rolodex full of business cards is not much use if no one returns your calls, or you find their diaries are mysteriously booked up whenever you want to meet them. You have to get beyond the ice-breaking stage promptly and start building a relationship.

Take care not to mistake alliances and business networks for friendship, even if you go out to company-sponsored social events together. Remember the dictum of Lord Palmerston, the 19th-century British prime minister, who said we 'have no permanent allies, only permanent interests'. In business, do not expect to have permanent allies, let alone permanent friends. Even your interests will change.

In this shifting and uncertain world, you need to anchor your relationships around mutual interest and mutual advantage. At the heart of building alliances is the need to build trust. Put simply: how far will you go to help someone you do not know or trust?

In building alliances, think of the trust equation:

$$T = (V \times C)/R$$

Exercise 4.11:
Building alliances and trust

Create a short list of the people whose support you most need, including your boss. For each one, build a trust profile to see how well connected you are with them. Use the trust equation above, where:

T = trust;
V = values intimacy.

You share the same goals, same values, same priorities and same outlook. You do not need to like them. You both talk the same talk. You can start building trust fast here, even if you have not met someone before. The goal is to find some area of common interest.

Networking starts with the heart, not the head. Find ways to engage them emotionally. For example:

- Let them talk about themselves (see Part 4, Section 10.1). Look interested. Flattery works.
- Find common colleagues ('Do you know so-and-so?').
- Find common business experiences to share: salespeople love swapping war stories, and so do most business people.
- Find common social interests.

If you are meeting them in their office, look around for vital signs. Real examples include:

- Pictures of lakes: 'How wonderful! Do you enjoy walking as well? In the Lake District? What a great place!'
- Professional qualifications on the wall: 'I see you got your degree from Harvard/Hull/Hamburg. What was that like?'
- A picture of a classic car: 'Is that yours? How long have you had it?'

For your own boss, you should be very clear about:

- How will the boss be measured and rewarded at the end of the year (his or her real interests)?
- What are the three major projects the boss is working on this year?
- What are the boss's career ambitions, and how will he or she fulfil them?
- What are the boss's personal interests, and do any intersect with yours?

Once you have engaged the heart, you can engage the head. To make the network work, you need to find some common interests where there is mutual advantage to working together. Go back to the selling skills section (Part 2, Section 3): try to discover a common problem or opportunity to work on together, with clear benefits to both sides.

C = credibility.

This is the extent to which you have credibility with each other: have you delivered the results and fulfilled promises to each other? Trust building normally starts with small promises and obligations, and then builds up to larger ones. 'C' is about being able to walk the talk. Small things count. After a meeting, send round a thank-you note or a summary of the meeting the same day. Speed impresses: it shows that you are both efficient and committed.

R = risk.

We often think of risk objectively: financial risk, health and safety risk, litigation risk, political risk. This is important, but it is a sideshow in building alliances, trust and networks. Real risk is personal risk.

Look at risk from your partner's perspective: how will this affect me, how much will it cost me, how much effort will it take and will I look good or bad if it succeeds or fails? The more you can do to reduce the perceived risk and effort for someone else, the more likely that person is to collaborate with you.

In building credibility, you will need to start on small and low-risk things so that confidence and credibility can build step by step. Ultimately, your network of alliances will be built one person at a time, one action at a time.

An old-fashioned Rolodex full of business cards is not much use if no one returns your calls.

Networking starts with the heart, not the head.

NOTES

Section 11
Time management

Time management is not about being busy. We are all too busy already, and there is an infinite amount of work to be done. It is about being effective with what time we have. There are many tips and techniques, like:

- Handle each piece of paper or e-mail only once.
- Do it right first time.
- Keep a clear desk for a clear mind (and hope you do not have a wooden desk...).

But let us make it simple. The following exercise, if practised, will make you more time-effective than most people.

Exercise 4.12:
Three ways to improve time management

1. *Decide what you really want and need to do.*
   This is the old-fashioned list of goals and priorities for the year, the month, the week and the day. Clear goal focus makes it easier to know what not to do, what to delegate and time traps to avoid. A simple test of time well spent is to ask: 'How will I remember this year in 20 years' time?' Rest assured, you will not remember this year for the number of e-mails you sent or the bonus you got. You will remember it for what you accomplished. If a year is too long to think about, then ask yourself: 'How will I remember this month at the end of the year?' You will not remember it for getting the expense report in on time, sending 620 e-mails and treading water.

2. *Find out what you actually do.*
   Keep an activity log for a few days. See how much relates to your priorities. Decide how much you can delegate, reduce or stop. If the 35-hour working week was really enforced, some people would have to spend at least 100 hours a week

in the office to do 35 hours of work, after eliminating breaks, internet time, personal calls, gossip, wasted meetings, lunch and planning the next holiday, office party or wedding.

3. *Create your prioritized To Do list for today, and follow it.* This should fall out of your goals list. ABC analysis (or red/yellow/green) is a simple way to prioritize your time and tasks so that you deal with the A-list before the B-list before the C-list (if ever). There is a trade-off between what is important and what is urgent. Fundamentalist followers of Covey say you should only focus on what is important: but then when do the urgent things get done? And if only the important things get done, we would have cars with engines but without radios, heaters, power steering, side windows and any creature comforts. Equally, if you only do the urgent things, then that is a recipe for being in a flat panic and firefighting all day. Ignore the rhetoric and theory from self-professed gurus: find a balance that works for you.

Keep a clear desk for a clear mind (and hope you do not have a wooden desk...).

You will not remember this year for the number of e-mails you sent.

NOTES

Section 12
Effective meetings

There are three tests of an effective meeting. You can use these tests to decide if you want to attend a meeting or hold a meeting and who you want to attend the meeting. Each participant in the meeting should be able to answer three questions at the end of the meeting:

■ What did I learn?
■ What did I contribute?
■ What do I do next?

If the participants have good answers for all three questions, it has been a good meeting for them. If they learned nothing, contributed nothing and do nothing next, it was a failure for them and they should not have been there.

These tests help you avoid the just-in-case syndrome and the face-time syndromes that convert a small meeting with the CEO into a major convention:

■ *Just-in-case*
Executives bring all their bag carriers with them, because the bag carriers did the work and know the answers. They are there just in case an awkward question is asked. If executives do not know the answers, they are in the wrong meeting and possibly in the wrong job.
■ *Face time*
Junior staff mistakenly believe that turning up at a meeting with the CEO and staying mute the whole time will impress the CEO. It does not. The CEO would rather staff were doing something useful with the organization's money.

Asking the three questions above sorts out those who need to be at the meeting from those who simply want to be at the meeting.

Exercise 4.13:
Questions for meetings

1. Next time you arrange a meeting, think through the three questions for each person attending. If people will not have good answers at the end, do not invite them.
2. Next time you go to a meeting, go with your own agenda structured around the three points. It may be that your only action point is to catch a hard-to-get person informally at the meeting. Do not blindly accept the given agenda: make sure you know what you want to get out of the meeting and what you will contribute as well.

If executives do not know the answers, they are in the wrong meeting and possibly in the wrong job.

NOTES

_____

_____

_____

_____

_____

_____

_____

_____

_____

Section 13
Projects

13.1 Projects: Principles

The outcomes of projects, like battles, are normally determined before they start. The wise leader invests heavily in starting the project right, before much time, money and effort are consumed across the organization.

Projects normally fail because they succumb to one of the four horsemen of the project apocalypse:

■ the wrong problem;
■ the wrong sponsor;
■ the wrong team;
■ the wrong process.

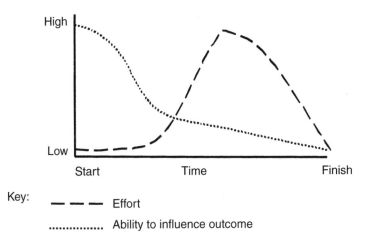

Figure 4.1 Projects: effort and potential to influence the outcome

Figure 4.1 shows that, the later you leave it, the harder it is to influence the final outcome. Heroic firefighting is futile near the end of the project: by then the outcome is largely determined and the effort has largely been spent. To ensure success, the leader must set the project up for success from the very start. Part 4, Section 13.2 looks at the major disasters to avoid: if you can avoid them then you are well on the way to success.

> **The outcomes of projects, like battles, are normally determined before they start.**

NOTES

_____

_____

_____

_____

_____

_____

_____

_____

_____

_____

_____

_____

_____

_____

_____

_____

13.2 Projects: The four horsemen of the apocalypse

The wrong problem

The right problem is someone's red issue. Three tests of a red issue:

- The stakes for failure and success are high, and you can measure them in financial or non-financial terms.
- The issue is not just important (solving climate change) but also urgent ('We will go bust next year if we don't...').
- The organization is already working on the problem, and is experiencing some setbacks. If no one is working on it, then is it really important and urgent?

The wrong sponsor

Someone must own the problem. That person will have the power and authority to implement the solution. A simple first test is to ask who needs to be involved in implementing the solution: the chances are that it will involve many people from across the organization. If the sponsor can bring these people together and get them to commit time, money and resource, he or she may be the right sponsor. A weak sponsor guarantees failure: he or she will not be able to remove the inevitable political roadblocks when the going gets tough.

The wrong team

Insist on the A-team. This is a fundamental test. If the project is important, they will put the A-team on it. The B-team is a sign that the project is not important and is a recipe for hell going forwards: it will never quite achieve the desired outcomes in the desired time to the desired quality, and it will keep on stumbling over hurdles that an A-team will leap over. The leader of a B-team will find that evenings, weekends and holidays disappear in a miasma of crises and chaos.

The wrong process

Most project planning gets hung up on this. If the first three horsemen of the apocalypse are avoided, then this one vanishes as well. But no amount of good process will save a project if the first three horsemen are wreaking havoc.

> **The leader of a B-team will find that evenings, weekends and holidays disappear in a miasma of crises and chaos.**

NOTES

_____

_____

_____

_____

_____

_____

_____

_____

_____

_____

_____

_____

_____

_____

13.3 Projects: Techniques

This is where geeks get very excited about Gantt and PERT charts and critical path analysis and come up with highly complex engineering-type diagrams that only they understand. Gantt and PERT charts are designed to help people who do not need help. The rest of humanity needs something simpler.

Design principles for a good project plan:

■ Do not start at the start. Start at the end with a very clear view of what needs to be achieved, summarized in 10 words maximum. If you start at the beginning you will never get to the finish.

■ Find the minimum number of steps required to get to the end: make it simple. This should show what critical steps happen in which order. Then create a timeline. Then drill down on each of the key steps to get as much detail as you wish.

■ Find some early wins to create momentum. People want instant gratification and to believe they are backing a winner.

Some classic project planning traps:

■ No clear deliverables, and conflicting expectations among stakeholders.

■ No clear staging posts where progress can be reviewed and measured against goals.

■ Excessive caution. If you need to do it, do it right and do it once. Investing just enough to lose is not smart. Running unrepresentative pilots and proofs of concept waste time and achieve nothing.

■ Process myopia. This is where the geeks fall in love with their process maps, risk logs, issues logs, meeting logs, telephone logs and master logs. The purpose of the project is to achieve an outcome, not run a perfect process.

■ Poor governance structure and process (see Part 4, Section 13.4).

Gantt and PERT charts are designed to help people who do not need help.

If you start at the beginning you will never get to the finish.

NOTES

_____

_____

_____

_____

_____

_____

_____

_____

_____

_____

_____

_____

_____

_____

_____

_____

_____

_____

13.4 Projects: Governance

Senior managers can get very excited about starting a project, and then lose interest in the hard grind of seeing it through. Good governance of a project is essential to its success.

The best way to let a project spin out of control, fail to deliver and cost a fortune is as follows:

1. Fail to put in formal governance procedures. Assume the consultants will do this for you.
2. Make decisions, when they are needed, slowly. Indecision kills projects and kills morale.
3. Change your mind quite often.

Good governance is not rocket science:

1. Have a clear governance structure. Create a RACI chart for the programme:
   - R = responsibilities. Who is responsible for delivering which part of the programme? There should be clear lines of accountability: it should be clear who gets praised or kicked at the end of the project, and for what.
   - A = authority. Who has ultimate authority for making decisions, approving budgets and reviewing progress? There should be only one authorizer per project. The authorizer also has ultimate accountability for the project. The authorizer is powerful and may not be involved day to day, but will call the project into existence and conclude it; in between, the authorizer may help remove political roadblocks and monitor progress.
   - C = cooperation. Whose cooperation is required and who needs to be consulted for what (eg finance may need to check your figures, but are not responsible for delivering the project)?
   - I = involvement. Who else needs to be involved (by providing expertise, assistance etc) or needs to be kept informed?

2. Have a clear governance process. The basics are easy, and normally ignored:
   - regular updates and review sessions;
   - standardized reports;
   - rapid and effective decision-making processes.

Indecision kills projects and kills morale.

NOTES

_____

_____

_____

_____

_____

_____

_____

_____

_____

_____

_____

_____

_____

_____

_____

Section 14
Managing change

14.1 Managing change: Are you ready to change?

Change is about people. Most sane people do not like change. Change involves hard work and risk:

■ Will I still have a job after the change?
■ Who will my boss be?
■ Will I need new skills?
■ Will I succeed?

So when you hear people object to change, you will hear very rational arguments against change. Listen behind the rational arguments and you will hear emotional fears and political objections to what you propose. Worst of all, you will hear the overwhelming silence of apathy: doing precisely nothing is the best way to defeat change.

The first test is to know if your organization is ready to change. Use the change equation to figure this out. Here it is in all its spurious mathematical accuracy. Change succeeds when:

$$N \times V \times C \times F > R$$

Exercise 4.14:
Is your organization ready for change?

Use the change equation to see how ready your team is for change:

■ N = need for change. How much pain and threat do people experience with the way things are at the moment?
■ V = vision of the end result. Does the team see the benefits of change?

- C = capability and credibility. Does the team have the capability to change, and do you have a successful track record of change?
- F = first steps. Are them some practical first steps that build momentum, achieve some early wins and build confidence?
- R = risks and costs of change. How large are the personal, political and financial costs of the change?

Repeat this exercise for each individual to see how ready he or she is personally to change, and repeat it for the organization as a whole.

Most sane people do not like change.

NOTES

_____

_____

_____

_____

_____

_____

_____

_____

_____

_____

_____

14.2 Managing change: The cycle of change

Change, unlike rivers, rarely runs smoothly. The initial burst of enthusiasm gets submerged in the trench warfare of detail, opposition and setbacks. You cannot eliminate these challenges. But you can at least set expectations so that no one is surprised by what happens.

The change cycle normally takes the following pattern (see Figure 4.2):

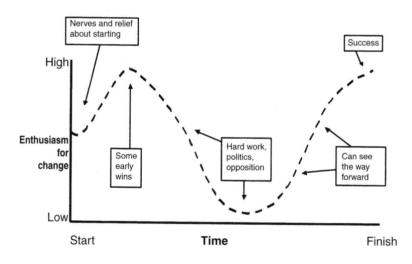

Figure 4.2 Change and the valley of death

■ *Stage one:* The enthusiasm of an early start with some early wins.

■ *Stage two:* The fall into despair as the challenges and the opposition mount.

- *Stage three:* The valley of death. This is where it seems that things cannot get worse. This stage can be good news: the opposition shows that people are engaging in the change and discovering its scale and importance. At this stage, the true leaders emerge: future-focused, solution-focused and action-focused, while everyone else is wallowing in a slough of despond.

- *Stage four:* The roller coaster moves back up as everyone else starts to see that success is possible. Enthusiasm builds the closer everyone gets to the finish line.

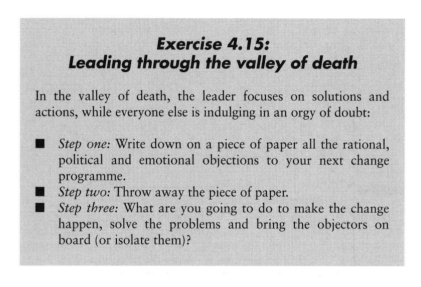

Exercise 4.15:
Leading through the valley of death

In the valley of death, the leader focuses on solutions and actions, while everyone else is indulging in an orgy of doubt:

- *Step one:* Write down on a piece of paper all the rational, political and emotional objections to your next change programme.
- *Step two:* Throw away the piece of paper.
- *Step three:* What are you going to do to make the change happen, solve the problems and bring the objectors on board (or isolate them)?

Remember, people reach levels of readiness for change at different times. Helping people adjust to change takes time.

> **The leader focuses on solutions and actions, while everyone else is indulging in an orgy of doubt.**

NOTES

Section 15
Reorganizing

15.1 Reorganizing: Rationale

Some people naively believe that reorganizations are about finding the perfect organization structure. Over the years, such naivety turns to cynicism as they see the corporate carousel turn full circle time and again: centralize and decentralize and back again; functional to product to geographic to customer focus and back again; another delayering, which only seems to add more layers and confusion.

In practice, a leader can use a reorganization to achieve three outcomes:

1. *Improve the organization structure.*
    This is in line with received wisdom. Changing conditions require changing responses, so no single organization structure will remain perfect for long.
2. *Change the balance of power.*
    Some leaders are like weak monarchs who are held to ransom by powerful barons. Moving the power barons around, with perhaps a ritual execution of one or two, has a powerful effect on the barons: they start to respect the power of the monarch and, cut off from their old fiefdoms, become more dependent on the patronage of the monarch. Every leader needs to put in place his or her preferred team: a reorganization is therefore as much about people and politics as it is about structure and logic.
3. *Reset expectations.*
    A reorganization is a perfect opportunity to change the psychological contract between the leader and individual team members. This is not just about performance goals: it is a two-way conversation about styles, how they should work together and what needs to change in future.

In theory, a leader reorganizes based on designing the right organization structure to support the corporate strategy. This is the rational method advocated by consultants. Back in the real world, most leaders reorganize intuitively the right way. They start by looking at the people they have, and then they work out how to deploy them to best effect. The result may be theoretically suboptimal, but it is practically the best thing to do.

> **Moving the power barons around, with perhaps a ritual execution of one or two, has a powerful effect.**

NOTES

_____

_____

_____

_____

_____

_____

_____

_____

_____

_____

_____

_____

_____

_____

15.2 Reorganizing: The need for speed

Reorganize fast. Reorganize once. Remove the uncertainty as fast as you can, and then focus on building the business.

The best time to reorganize is when you start in a new position. Most CEOs alter their top team when they are appointed. There are three reasons for this:

■ They put the right leadership team in place as soon as possible: a dysfunctional leadership team is not good for the organization.
■ They minimize the FUD factor: fear, uncertainty and doubt. The longer you leave it, the more the FUD factor rises, politicking rises and morale collapses.
■ They avoid getting trapped in the old ways and the old psychological contract. It makes change, not stability, the way of life.

Speed is particularly important when 'letting people go'. If you have to kill someone, at least be humane and do it fast. The legal fetish for due process simply spins the agony out for everyone: the victim hangs on desperately for the last breath of corporate air; the executioner boss feels in turn embarrassed, frustrated, angry and sympathetic; the organization is transfixed by the trauma being played out. Move the person out as fast as you can. Then focus your efforts on the survivors: they are your future. They need to be assured that you are not continuing to swing your axe randomly: they need to focus on doing a good job, rather than jockeying for survival.

If you have to kill someone, at least be humane and do it fast.

NOTES

Section 16
Creating a vision

16.1 Creating a vision: For teams

Visions are not just for mystics and chief executives. Team leaders need to give their team a vision. At its simplest, a compelling vision has three elements:

■ Here is the worthwhile goal we are chasing.
■ Here is your important role in helping us get there.
■ Here is how we can get there together.

Note that the vision is not just about you: it has to be made relevant to each individual. People want to know they are doing something worthwhile, that their contribution is important and that success is possible. If your vision does these things, it will be powerful.

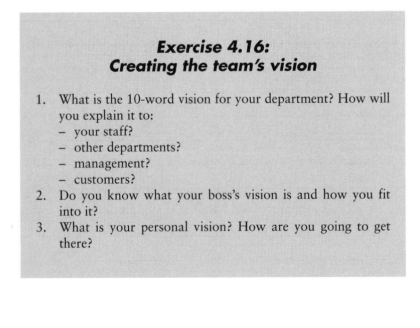

Exercise 4.16:
Creating the team's vision

1. What is the 10-word vision for your department? How will you explain it to:
   – your staff?
   – other departments?
   – management?
   – customers?
2. Do you know what your boss's vision is and how you fit into it?
3. What is your personal vision? How are you going to get there?

> **People want to know they are doing something worthwhile, that their contribution is important and that success is possible.**

NOTES

_____

_____

_____

_____

_____

_____

_____

_____

_____

_____

_____

_____

_____

_____

_____

_____

_____

_____

_____

_____

_____

_____

16.2 Creating a vision: For the whole organization

When creating a vision, remember RUSS. RUSS represents the four elements of a strong vision:

■ *Relevant*
The vision should be relevant to the current context and challenges of the organization. It should also be made relevant to each stakeholder in the organization.
■ *Unique*
You could not (easily) substitute the name of any other organization into the vision: it is unique to the strengths and aspirations of the one organization.
■ *Stretching*
The vision should be more than business as usual. It should have an element of stretch in it. This will help managers understand priorities and focus their efforts: it will help them understand what they should do and what they should not do.
■ *Simple*
If a vision is not simple, it will not be remembered. And if no one remembers your vision, it is unlikely that they are going to be able to act on it.

A classic vision: NASA

John F Kennedy famously announced a mission: 'to put a man on the moon and bring him back alive again, by the end of this decade'. This was the mission impossible that led to the creation of NASA. On 16 July 1969, mission impossible was accomplished.

Put the NASA vision to the RUSS test:

■ *Relevant*
This was about beating the Russians in space: the Russians had already put the first satellite into space (sputnik) and the first cosmonaut (Yuri Gagarin). The United States was losing

the Cold War in terms of technology, prestige and the race for the last frontier. It was a must-win battle for the nation.

■ *Unique*
It would be hard to claim that a moon landing was the vision for Procter & Gamble or Shell: it was a truly unique vision.

■ *Stretching*
At the time, no one knew if the vision was possible or if the technology could be developed: it was a huge stretch.

■ *Simple*
Everyone could remember it.

The power of the vision was compelling: it galvanized political, financial and technical support. It kept NASA focused so that setbacks like some of the Gemini disasters did not destroy the programme. Then look at what happened when the vision was achieved: NASA lost its way. It may have a vision now, but not everyone knows it. It has had some successes (the Hubble telescope) but the setbacks tend to set it back a long way (the Shuttle disaster).

Now compare your organization's vision with NASA's: does it have the RUSS values of NASA pre-1969 or post-1969?

Exercise 4.17:
Creating the organization's vision

■ Create a 10-word vision for Microsoft's shareholders and employees, for example. Create another 10-word vision for Microsoft's regulators and customers, for example.
■ Test your company's vision against the criteria above.
■ Create a 10-word vision for your company, again looking at how it might alter for different stakeholder groups.

If a vision is not simple, it will not be remembered.

NOTES

Part 5

Values and behaviours

Section 1
Becoming a leader people want to follow

As a leader, you will have many people who have to follow you. The challenge for the leader is this: 'Why would anyone want to follow you?' Many leaders make the fatal mistake of thinking that, because they have followers, people want to follow them. In reality, followers put up with abysmal leaders because the costs and risks of trying to leave the organization they are in are too high. Leaders should never mistake compliance for commitment.

You will have seen an extended version of the list below in Table 1.3, which looks at the expectations of leaders at all levels. The list below shows what people look for in top leaders. In brackets, it shows how satisfied they are with their leaders:

■ vision (61%);
■ ability to motivate others (37%);
■ decisiveness (47%);
■ ability to handle crises (56%);
■ honesty and integrity (48%).

Note the following:

■ Most of the expectations of leaders are simple, and can be learned.
■ There is a very large expectation gap around motivation (Part 2, Section 2).
■ Smaller expectation gaps exist around honesty and integrity (Part 5, Section 7), decisiveness (Part 4, Section 8) and ability to handle crises (Part 3, Sections 2 and 3).
■ Vision (Part 4, Section 16) is most important, and is the area where people are most satisfied.

Note also what is missing from this list: you do not have to be a charismatic superhero to lead. This is just as well: short of getting a charisma transplant, there is no known way of training for charisma. Most of the leaders in our research programme could not be described as charismatic: they did not need to be. By delivering against the five basic expectations above, they were able to create a loyal band of followers.

Why would anyone want to follow you?

There is no known way of training for charisma.

NOTES

_____

_____

_____

_____

_____

_____

_____

_____

_____

_____

_____

_____

_____

_____

Section 2
Working to win

Athletes, like leaders, do not win by playing to their weaknesses and imagining failure. They win by building on their strengths and rehearsing, visualizing success in their minds. Leaders have an advantage over athletes: leaders can delegate other people to look after their weaknesses.

From this come four simple principles of working to win:

1. *Play to your strengths.*
    Know what you are good at and in what context (occupation, company and project).
2. *Visualize success.*
    This is important before big, stressful events. Walk through each step of the event seeing what a successful outcome looks like, feels like, smells like and sounds like. Rehearse it as vividly as possible. Then make it happen.
3. *Think like a winner.*
    Remember all the times you have done great things. Let yourself get back into that frame of mind. When you believe you will succeed, you will. Failure is a self-fulfilling prophecy. If you have no enthusiasm or confidence, no one else will be enthusiastic or confident for you.
4. *Create a team that compensates for your weaknesses.*
    If you are no good at accounting, rest assured there are thousands of accountants out there to help.

Exercise 5.1:
Learning to work to win

1. Draw up your list of strengths and weaknesses. See what you can do to work in situations that play to your strengths, and start looking for people you can partner with to compensate for your weaknesses.

2. Try visualizing success and rehearsing as vividly as possible the sights, sounds, smells, feelings and actions of success.
3. Visualize your biggest successes as vividly as possible. These successes define who you are. You are a winner, so keep winning.

Failure is a self-fulfilling prophecy.

If you have no enthusiasm or confidence, no one else will be enthusiastic or confident for you.

NOTES

_____

_____

_____

_____

_____

_____

_____

_____

_____

_____

_____

Section 3
Learning to be lucky

All successful leaders admit to being lucky: they create their own luck. The question is how to create your own luck. Try the 4P luck programme:

1. *Practice*
   The more you practise, the luckier you get. The long-shot putt becomes a 50/50 putt; the 50/50 becomes easy. Practice converts luck into skill.
2. *Persistence*
   The difference between failure and success is giving up. Setbacks are great learning experiences: most leaders and entrepreneurs have more than their share of setbacks.
3. *Preparation*
   If you do not know what you are looking for, you will not find it. Know what you want; hunt it persistently.
4. *Positive outlook*
   Look for solutions, not problems. Look for action, not analysis. Be confident in yourself: if you are not enthusiastic, no one else will be. Don't get sucked into a culture of negativity.

All this means that luck can be learned.

Exercise 5.2:
Focus on luck

1. Review all the setbacks you have had. Are you lucky? Review all the successes and narrow escapes you have had. Are you still unlucky? Luck is largely a matter of self-perception.
2. Look at all the problems you have. Feeling bad? Look at all the options you have and how you might achieve them.

Feeling better? Now find some practical first steps and move to action.

3. Look at some successful entrepreneurs. Aren't their ideas obvious? You or I could have done it as well. The entrepreneurs do not even look smart intellectually or socially. So I must be able to do better than them. Right now, someone is making the next obvious idea into a big success. Why shouldn't that person be you?

Leaders create their own luck.

NOTES

Section 4
Positive leadership

Cynicism is in plentiful supply in the lower reaches of many organizations. There are many cynical junior and middle managers who are going to stay that way: cynical and junior. Our research found no effective leaders who were cynical about their work, their organization, themselves or their lives. They were relentlessly positive about everything.

Being positive is different from the hippy mantra of 'Be happy; don't worry.' Positive leadership is a frame of mind where leaders:

▪ look to the future, not to the past;
▪ focus on action, not on analysis;
▪ see possibilities, not just problems;
▪ take control versus being controlled;
▪ create options versus accept the status quo.

Some people behave like this naturally. For the rest of us, the good news is that these are habits that can be learned. Choose which set of questions from Table 5.1 you want, in a tough situation, to be working on in your head.

Table 5.1 Asking the right questions

Leader Mindset	Follower Mindset
What are some possible solutions/options/ways fowrard?	What went wrong?
What can I do now to regain control and build momentum?	Why have I been put in this position?
Whose support do I need and how will I get it?	Who messed up? Who is going to put this right?
What can I learn from this?	How do I avoid the blame?

Keep asking yourself these questions and you will run a serious risk of appearing and acting like a positive and effective leader.

In our research we came across some outstanding examples of leaders thinking positively:

■ An arsonist had burned down one wing of the school. The head teacher saw this as a great opportunity to redesign and rebuild the school in the way she wanted it to be, and the insurance company would pay. She was not, as far as we know, responsible for the arson attack.

■ The Japanese subsidiary of a multinational was losing $2 million a year and jobs were at risk. The leader of the subsidiary persuaded head office that it should invest $2 million a year in building its Japanese subsidiary. Head office thought this was great. Losses (bad) were miraculously converted into investment (good) and everyone was happy.

■ The politician was meeting voters, and always wanted to say something nice to them. One person came up and introduced himself as a pawnbroker: what can you say positive about that? 'Wonderful... pawnbroking is where banking really started hundreds of years ago... and you are still the only people who provide banking services to the poor. You provide a very important and historic service.' One more vote in the bag as the pawnbroker disappeared, happy, down the street.

> **Cynical junior and middle managers are going to stay that way: cynical and junior.**

NOTES

_____

_____

_____

Section 5
Professional leadership

'Professionalism' is in danger of becoming a dirty word. The dirtiest foul in football is the professional foul. Then there are professional politicians. And of course the *Titanic* was built by professionals, whereas the Ark was built by an amateur. In the business world, 'lack of professionalism' has become a lazy accusation levelled against subordinates whose style we do not like. It is vague and insulting in equal proportions.

Professionalism is important, and it varies in each context. It is important to figure out what it means and for everyone to agree. As an exercise, draw your team together to define what 'professionalism' means. An easy way to start is to identify unprofessional behaviour. Draw up your own list of pet hates, and then make sure you do not fall into those traps. Typical traps include:

■ mobile phones ringing in meetings;
■ being late for meetings;
■ bad-mouthing customers;
■ talking about business or customers in public spaces;
■ failing to follow up on promises;
■ ignoring the dress code.

Once you and your team have created the long list, get the team to vote and identify the four or five most important areas to focus on: these will be the traps that are most often fallen into. Then agree to enforce those areas. Trying to enforce a list of 57 varieties of unprofessional behaviour becomes a legalistic and bureaucratic nightmare. Everyone can remember and focus on a few key areas of professional behaviour. Once those behaviours are established, over a few months, you can move on to the next set of behaviours.

> **The *Titanic* was built by professionals, whereas the Ark was built by an amateur.**

NOTES

Section 6
Etiquette

Business etiquette is not about knowing how to use fish knives. It is about creating an environment where you can get the most out of other people. For some leaders, this means creating an atmosphere of stress, tension, bullying and blame. They think this is dynamic. There is a better way of getting the best out of people.

How well do you react when someone keeps you waiting, answers phone calls during your meeting, forgets your name, dresses badly, has not washed, puts his feet up on the table and starts swearing?

The principle of etiquette is the Golden Rule: 'Do unto others as you would have them do unto you.'

Exercise 5.3:
Etiquette that works for you

Create a hit list of the small things people do that annoy you. Create another list of small things people have done to please you. The two are the basis of your 'do and don't do' etiquette guide.

Naturally, different cultures do things differently. But, even in Japan, you will not go too far wrong if people see you are making an effort and showing goodwill.

Making a friend costs little. Losing a friend can be ruinous.

Do unto others as you would have them do unto you.

NOTES

_____

_____

_____

_____

_____

_____

_____

_____

_____

_____

_____

_____

_____

_____

_____

_____

_____

_____

_____

_____

_____

_____

_____

_____

Section 7
Honesty

For a leader, honesty is not just about morals and ethics. It is much more important than that. Honesty is about survival.

Exercise 5.4:
Who wants to work for you?

Think back over the leaders you have wanted to work for, versus those you have had to work for. How many of the leaders you have wanted to work for did you not trust? The chances are, you trust the leaders you work for. And you probably only trust people who are honest with you.

If people have to follow you because of your power and position, they will. But do not be fooled into thinking they want to follow you unless they trust you.

To build trust with your followers, you have to be honest with them. This is hard-form honesty: telling the whole truth promptly, even when it is painful. This is an honesty test most politicians fail; then they wonder why no one trusts them.

Exercise 5.5:
Honesty is tough

- Someone is not meeting your expectations. Do you tell the person now or let it slide in the hope that things might get better anyway?
- The business is facing difficulties. Do you tell the staff or keep quiet because bad news might unsettle them?

In each case, failing to act promptly simply builds up bigger problems for later, and failure to act is corrosive of the trust you need to build.

Honesty is not just about morals and ethics. It is about survival.

NOTES

_____

_____

_____

_____

_____

_____

_____

_____

_____

_____

_____

_____

_____

_____

_____

Section 8
Humility

The humble leader is an oxymoron, in the same league as Microsoft Works, Civil Service and friendly fire (or airline food, briefings, government organization, holy war, half-naked, non-working mother, social services, tax return and United Nations). Humility for leaders is not about cleaning out the toilets to show you can do it.

Humility for leaders is about self-awareness. Effective leaders are keenly aware of what they are good at and what they are not good at. It takes great self-confidence, self-awareness and humility to admit to not being good at things. But that is the critical first step towards doing something about it.

All leaders have weaknesses: none get ticks in all the boxes. But fortunately, leadership is a team sport. The first act of a good leader should be to assemble a good team. An ineffective team will all be clones of the leader. An effective team will complement the leader's technical strengths and personal style.

Exercise 5.6:
Developing self-awareness

Make an honest (and humble) list of what you are good at and what you are not good at in terms of:

■ technical skills;
■ interpersonal and leadership skills;
■ personal style.

Now have someone you know and trust review the list with you. You can do the same for the other person and make it a two-way exercise. Finally, review the strengths and weaknesses of your team: have you got the balance right?

It takes great self-confidence, self-awareness and humility to admit to not being good at things.

No leader gets ticks in all the boxes.

NOTES

_____

_____

_____

_____

_____

_____

_____

_____

_____

_____

_____

_____

_____

_____

_____

_____

_____

Section 9
Living the values

Leaders have more power than even they realize. People take their cue from your behaviour. Your little personal cloud of gloom can spread into a major depression across the office. As a leader, you can decide what are the values you want to leave as a legacy.

There are two ways you can build the values.

The obvious way is through the performance, measurement and promotion systems. If you pay call-centre staff by the number of calls they process, expect volume not quality. If you promote a great salesperson with questionable ethics, people will read the message loud and clear.

The second way you build the values is through your behaviour. Do not expect commitment to your cost-cutting programme if you arrive to make the announcement in your private jet. People look not just at what you do, but at how you do it. In the leadership goldfish bowl, you are under constant surveillance. You are a show, so make the most of it.

Exercise 5.7:
Leaving a legacy

Note down the values you would like to leave behind:

∎ How can you demonstrate those values in any of the following: a budget meeting, a performance review, a coaching session?
∎ How well do the promotion, measurement and bonus systems reflect those values?
∎ What are the real rules of success and failure in your organization (see Part 1, Section 4) and how far do they match with the values you want to leave behind?
∎ What are the values your peers display?

In the leadership goldfish bowl, you are under constant surveillance.

NOTES

_____

_____

_____

_____

_____

_____

_____

_____

_____

_____

_____

_____

_____

_____

_____

_____

_____

_____

_____

Section 10
Ambition

Leaders are ambitious, for themselves and for their organizations. Managers may be reasonable. Leaders are, selectively, unreasonable. People remember Alexander the Great, not his kid brother Alexander the Reasonable.

Reasonable managers understand why the profit target needs to be adjusted down: suppliers' costs go up, salaries go up, regulators and tax inspectors demand more, competition intensifies and customers are pushing down prices. So of course the profit target is unreasonable.

Unreasonable leaders listen to all the reasons why something cannot be achieved. Then they simply focus on how it will be achieved.

No reasonable leader would have taken on IBM, UPS, the BBC, Delta/American/United or Ford and General Motors. Reasonable leaders did not start Dell, FedEx, CNN/Sky, Southwest Airlines or Honda and Toyota. They all had nothing to start with, but successfully challenged huge incumbents.

Whether you are running an empire, a business or a team you can still decide whether to take the low road of reasonableness or the high road of ambition, stretch and unreasonableness.

Leaders with ambition tend to enjoy accelerated careers: they succeed fast or fail fast. But at least they learn a lot and the journey is exciting. Which road will you take?

Exercise 5.8:
Reaching for the moon

■ How do you want to remember this year in 20 years' time?
■ Where do you really want to be in 10 years' time?
■ Are your answers consistent with what you are doing now?

Take the low road of reasonableness or the high road of ambition.

NOTES

_____

_____

_____

_____

_____

_____

_____

_____

_____

_____

_____

_____

_____

_____

_____

_____

_____

_____

_____

Section 11
Hard work

Actors recognize that it can take 20 years of hard grind to become an overnight success. The same is true of the leadership journey: it is seriously hard work.

Telling people to work hard is not very inspirational. So the issue is different: how do people sustain the level of effort required to succeed?

Look at any successful actor, sports star or leader. How many of them dislike what they do? In reality, you can only excel at what you enjoy; you can only sustain the hard work for success if you enjoy what you are doing. At this point, you may choose to look in dismay at those people who actually enjoy going to the workplace and working. That may be a hint about who has the stamina and commitment for the leadership journey.

The test for the emerging leader is the extent to which they enjoy what they are doing.

Exercise 5.9:
Enjoying hard work?

Answer a few simple questions about what you are doing:

■ Do you look forward to work in the morning?
■ Do you feel energized or drained of energy at work?
■ Are work challenges exciting or dispiriting?
■ Do you feel you are doing something worthwhile?
■ Are you optimistic or fearful about your future?
■ At the end of the day are you tired and irritable?
■ When do you feel the most enjoyment?

Every leader succeeds in context. The challenge is to make sure you are working in a context where the answers to the questions above are likely to be positive.

> **It can take 20 years of hard grind to become an overnight success.**

NOTES

Section 12
Learning and renewal

Over the years we all develop our ideas of what works for us. This is good. We need to discover the rules of survival and success in our context. But it is also the road to ruin. We all tend to get fixed with our ideas about what works. As long as our worlds do not change, then we do not need to change. But our worlds change all the time. Technology, markets, customers and staff are changing the rules of the game all the time. As with the tide ebbing and flowing, we may not notice it at first. But then we wake up one day and find that we are stranded by the receding tide. As we rise through an organization, the demands and expectations on us change. As CEOs, we face one set of demands when we are growing the business. Another set of skills is needed in a recession, when customers have tightened their wallets, markets are shrinking and competition has become a vicious fight for survival.

We cannot stand still and let the world run ahead of us.

Personal growth and professional growth tend to go hand in hand. A simple test is to ask an executive, or ask yourself, some simple questions:

■ What is your favourite music? If it is all Debbie Harry, Eurythmics, Dire Straits and Kate Bush then you are stuck in a 1980s time warp. If your favourite group is Oasis, keep very quiet about it. Musical taste dates executives as accurately as radiocarbon testing dates old fossils.
■ What are your all-time favourite films, film stars and books?
■ What are the most influential management books and articles you have read?

The other sin is to be a slave to fashion. If your vote for the greatest-ever Briton goes to David Beckham or Princess Diana, you are probably a fashion slave who will turn to every latest management fad in the belief that it is the coolest, sexiest transformational beast on the block. A little perspective helps identify fads for what they are.

You need to strike a balance between being a fossilized fool and being a fashion freak. This book cannot help you with your taste in music or films, but it can with management. At the end of the book is some suggested further reading, from ancient books to recent publications. But you have already taken the most important step: you have read this book.

> **If your favourite group is Oasis, keep very quiet about it.**

Musical taste dates executives as accurately as radiocarbon testing dates old fossils.

NOTES

_____

_____

_____

_____

_____

_____

_____

_____

_____

_____

_____

_____

_____

Section 13
Learning to lead

We come to the end of our journey where we started it: by making sure we ask and answer the right question. You will find many people trying to explain 'What is leadership?' That is the wrong question, because leadership is contextual: it depends on who you are and what your situation is. By far the more interesting question is 'How can I learn to lead?' If you cannot learn to lead, you cannot lead.

Your formal education has probably taught you precisely the wrong lessons in preparing you for leadership. Your employer has probably not helped either. As Part 1, Section 5 noted, school teaches us to work by ourselves on tasks we have been set and to produce a rational answer. Anyone who thinks that leadership is about working alone on pre-assigned tasks to achieve rational answers is going to be deeply disappointed.

Business school does not help: it teaches explicit knowledge like strategy, finance and accounting. You can be the world's best accountant and have the leadership potential of a jelly bean. Leadership skills are tacit skills: know-how more than know-what. Tacit skills have to be learned, not taught.

Business training rarely helps. Business training focuses on one or other of the following:

■ *Technical training*. This is about the craft skills of the job, for example bond trading and audit practice. At least these skills are practical and valued by participants.
■ *Soft skills*. This is where leaders run a mile. To go on training courses around people management sounds like they have been identified with weaknesses: leaders find it tough to admit to basic weaknesses in public. And the quality of much of the training gives them plenty of reason to discover that their diaries are mysteriously full whenever such training is being run.

We asked leaders how they had learned to lead. We gave them the following choices:

- books;
- courses;
- experience;
- role models;
- peers;
- bosses.

Not one said they had learned from books or courses (perhaps because this book was not available at the time). In that one reply, the whole leadership training industry disappears in a puff of irrelevance.

In practice, you will learn your leadership skills and style from some mix of experience, bosses, peers and role models. You will learn as much from the negative as you will from the positive examples. You will beg, borrow and steal pieces of leadership DNA from all around you to create your own unique profile.

This journey of discovery can be a random walk through miscellaneous experiences and colleagues. A random walk is not the best route to leadership. You need to be able to structure and accelerate your personal journey of discovery. That is where this book comes in. It does not claim to give all the answers to everything: the only good answers are ones that work for you. Instead, the book gives you a series of frameworks to use, to test and to help you observe better how leaders lead. It gives you a structure that will help accelerate your process of learning and discovery.

Whatever your journey is, enjoy it.

NOTES

Further reading

Books

Baylis, Nick (2005) *Learning from Wonderful Lives*, Wellbeing Press, Cambridge

Bennis, Warren (1989) *On Becoming a Leader*, Addison-Wesley, Reading, MA

Briggs Myers, Isabel (1995) *Gifts Differing: Understanding personality type*, Davies-Black, Mountain View, CA

Carnegie, Dale (1994) *How to Win Friends and Influence People*, Hutchinson, London

Collins, Jim (2001) *Good to Great*, Random House Business Books, London

Covey, S (1992) *The Seven Habits of Highly Effective People*, Simon & Schuster, London

Hesselbein, Frances and Cohen, Paul M (eds) (1999) *Leader to Leader*, Jossey Bass, San Francisco, CA

Holmes, Andrew and Wilson, Dan (2004) *Pains in the Office*, Capstone, Oxford

Huppert, FA, Baylis, NVK and Keverne, EB (2005) *The Science of Wellbeing*, Oxford University Press, Oxford

Johnson, Spencer (1999) *Who Moved my Cheese?*, Vermilion, London

Kotter, John (1988) *The Leadership Factor*, Free Press, New York

Landsberg, Max (2000) *The Tools of Leadership*, HarperCollins, London

Lees, John (2004) *How to Get a Job You'll Love*, McGraw-Hill, Maidenhead

Machiavelli, N (1961) *The Prince*, Penguin Books, London

Minto, Barbara (2005) *The Pyramid Principle*, Financial Times Prentice Hall, London

Nelson, Bob (2005) *1001 Ways to Reward Employees*, Workman, New York

Nelson Bolles, Richard (2004) *What Color Is Your Parachute?*, Ten Speed Press, Berkeley, CA

Owen, Jo (2005) *How to Lead*, Prentice Hall, Harlow

Owen, Jo (2006) *Management Stripped Bare*, 2nd edn, Kogan Page, London

Peters, Thomas J and Waterman, Jr, Robert H (1982) *In Search of Excellence*, Harper & Row, New York

Senge, Peter (1992) *The Fifth Discipline*, Random House, London

Sun Tzu (2003) *The Art of War*, Running Press Miniature Editions, Philadelphia, PA

Timpson, John (2002) *How to Be a Great Boss: The Timpson way*, Timpson Ltd, Manchester

Wiseman, Richard (2003) *The Luck Factor*, Arrow Books, London

Harvard Business Review

Cialdini, Robert (2001) *Harnessing the Science of Persuasion*, HBR OnPoint Collection

Gabarro, John J and Kotter, John P (1993) Managing your boss, May–June

Goleman, Daniel (1998) What makes an effective leader, Nov–Dec

Goleman, Daniel (2000) Leadership that gets results, Mar–Apr

Kotter, John (1999) What effective general managers really do, Mar

Zaleznik, Abraham, Mintzberg, Henry and Gosling, Jonathan (2003) *Your Best Managers Lead and Manage*, HBR OnPoint Collection

Websites

Count Kostov (use and abuse of numbers): www.countkostov.blogspot.com

Desert exercise: www.wilderdom.com/games/descriptions/SurvivalScenarios.html

Keirsey (good detail on MBTI): http://www.keirsey.com/

Myers-Briggs: http://www.myersbriggs.org/

Nick Baylis (excellent on personal well-being): http://www.nick-baylis.com/

Self-testing psychometrics (free tests): www.similarminds.com

Self-testing psychometrics (part of British Psychological Society): www.psychtesting.org.uk

Two fun sites for personality analysis: www.colorquiz.com; www.colorgenics.com

Index